MW00653495

God's Abode with Man

Os Justi Studies in Catholic Tradition

General Editor: Peter A. Kwasniewski

1 • J. Joy, *Disputed Questions on Papal Infallibility*

2 • R.-M. Rivoire, *Does "Traditionis Custodes" Pass the Juridical Rationality Test?*

3 • J. Shaw, *The Liturgy, the Family, and the Crisis of Modernity*

4 • P. Kwasniewski (ed.), *Illusions of Reform*

5 • G. Steckler, *The Triumph of Romanticism*

6 • T. Crean, *"Letters from that City…": A Guide to Holy Scripture for Students of Theology*

7 • S. Lanzetta, *God's Abode with Man: The Mystery of Divine Grace*

God's Abode with Man

The Mystery of Divine Grace

Fr. Serafino M. Lanzetta

OS JUSTI PRESS

Lincoln, Nebraska

Copyright © 2023 by Os Justi Press

All rights reserved.

No part of this book may be reproduced, stored in a retrieval
system, or transmitted in any form, or by any means, electronic,
mechanical, photocopying, or otherwise, without the prior
written permission of the publisher, except by a reviewer, who
may quote brief passages in a review.

Os Justi Press
P.O. Box 21814
Lincoln, NE 68542
www.osjustipress.com

Send inquiries to
info@osjustipress.com

ISBN 978-1-960711-34-2 (paperback)
ISBN 978-1-960711-35-9 (hardcover)
ISBN 978-1-960711-36-6 (eBook)

Typesetting by Nora Malone
Cover design by Julian Kwasniewski
On the cover: Simon Bening, *Villagers on Their
Way to Church* (c. 1550), tempera and gold
on parchment. Wikimedia Commons.

To my sister Caterina

*Man has received the command
to become God by grace.*

St. Basil the Great

Contents

Introduction: The Mystery of Divine Grace—
God's Gift That Makes Us Lovers 1

1. Grace in Divine Revelation 9
   The Mystery of Divine Grace in the Sacred Scriptures . . 9
      1. God's Grace in the Mystery of Creation 9
      2. Grace under a Covenantal Form 12
      3. Grace in the New Testament:
         A New Life in Christ 14
         3.1. Grace as a Gift of the Father 16
         3.2. Grace as a New Life. 16
         3.3. Grace as the Presence of the Holy Trinity . 21
   The Mystery of Divine Grace
   in the Fathers of the Church 23
      1. Grace in the Greek Fathers 23
      2. Grace in the Western Church. St. Augustine
         and the Problem of Pelagius. 26

2. God the Giver and Grace as a Divine Gift 35
   The Universal Salvific Will of God. 35
   Predestination as Choice and Love Ahead of Time . . . 38
      1. Predestination as Understood by Theologians
         over the Centuries 40
      2. The Dispute "De Auxiliis" Concerning
         the Activity of Grace and Free Will 46
      3. Grace and Free Will: A Mystery of
         Mutual Cooperation 50
   The Mystery of Non-Election or Reprobation. 54

3. Justification as the Happening and Realization
   of Divine Grace 59
   Justification as a Divine Process 60
   Martin Luther's View on Justification 63

The Answer of the Council of Trent 70
    1. Justification Is Gratuitous through Faith 71
    2. Faith Not Informed and the Doctrine of Merit. . 72
Sanctifying Grace as a Created, Interior,
  and Permanent Entity. 74
Sanctifying Grace as Participation in the Divine Nature
  and Inhabitation of the Holy Trinity 78
    1. Partakers of the Divine Nature 79
    2. The Inhabitation of the Triune God 81
Only through Baptism, Children of God 84

4. Grace from the Perspective of the Receiver:
  Actual Grace and Its Implications 89
  Actual Grace 90
  Divisions of Actual Grace 92
  Grace Perfects Human Nature. 94
  Grace and Glory 99
  Can Grace Be Experienced? 101
  The Grace of the Holy Spirit. 103
  Grace and Charity 106

5. Two Emblematic Positions on Grace,
  Both Heterodox 113
  Henri de Lubac: Grace Comes with Nature 114
  Karl Rahner: Grace Is in Nature
    as Nature Is Necessarily Open to Grace. 119
  A Way Forward: The Classic Distinction
    and Interdependence of Nature and Grace 130

Conclusion "Hail, Full of Grace!" 133

Introduction

The Mystery of Divine Grace— God's Gift That Makes Us Lovers

THERE IS ONLY ONE POSSIBLE WAY for God to be with us, to abide with man, and that is through the gift of His grace. The crucial question of Solomon, that sigh begging the heavens to rend and let God come down (cf. 1 King 8:27 and Is 64:1)—can God abide on earth, can His presence fill this holy Temple?—has been answered in Christ, the one through whom all graces flow. He is the true temple, God's living presence among us. The one who loves Him will be loved by His Father, and the Triune God will come to him to make their "abode" with him (cf. Jn 14:24, or, to make their "room" or "monastery"—*monén*—with him). Divine love produces the mystery of the inhabitation of the Most Holy Trinity in the soul through the inherent gift of divine grace. Grace is the condition to be with God, to become His living abode on earth, just as the grace of the Hypostatic Union in Christ, the very source of grace, is the condition for the Incarnation of God and for His "tangible" presence among us. Love makes us partakers of grace as grace is the fruit of divine love.

God's Abode with Man

Divine grace is indeed at the heart of Christian life. It is the Good News, the Gospel of salvation that we receive, as well as the greatest inward gift enabling us to listen to this News and to open up our hearts to welcome it. God gives us eternal life in His Son and makes us able to receive it in abundance.

Divine grace presents itself under various aspects. If we consider it firstly from the perspective of the Giver, we discover that grace is a favor granted by God. If we consider divine grace in itself, we discover that it is a gift. Originating from the Latin word *gratia* it means something that we do not pay for, something given out of pure love and benevolence. Lastly, if we consider it from the point of view of the recipient, we discover that it is the way we are sanctified and made grateful as children of God; it is the gift that transforms one's life. Grace is indeed a profound mystery—a mystery concerning the adhesion of a created entity (the soul in the state of grace) with an uncreated mystery, the Holy Spirit, the Sanctifier. Grace makes present in us the Holy Spirit, and consequently realizes the inhabitation of the Most Holy Trinity within us.

Divine grace is the beginning of a new life, a life created anew in Christ through baptism. As our Lord discloses, if we are not *reborn* in Christ and *remain* in Him, we cannot see God and have eternal life (see Jn 3:3–8; 15:4–9). In this way, divine grace—also called "sanctifying" or "habitual" grace—is our means of participating in the divine life of God, elevating us to a new status of life—one of divine filiation. As children of the heavenly Father, we are, at last, capable of enjoying the true freedom of remaining in the truth of Christ, living in the love of the Holy Spirit.

We also speak of grace as that operation by which God continually aids us. This *actual grace*, whilst respecting our nature, precedes, accompanies, and follows our actions, assisting our elevation to the supernatural realm. Raised above our natural domain, it becomes for us a source of an eternal reward—a supernatural merit.

Although grace essentially is one and indivisible, we may make distinctions to help us understand how it affects us. Sanctifying grace effects a deep and interior transformation of oneself, uniting one to God, whereas actual grace accompanies all of man's actions, assisting him to live righteously—the one adhering to the soul while the other operates momentarily. This interrelation between sanctifying grace and actual grace is shown by the Apostle St. Paul, who declares, "By the grace of God, I am what I am" (1 Cor 15:10), indicating the mystery of grace as the principle of transformation and sanctification. In hearing from our Lord that "[His] grace is sufficient for [him]: for power is made perfect in infirmity" (2 Cor 2:9), the Apostle refers to grace in its strengthening operation.

Grace ultimately perfects human nature—that nature which is the foundation for the activity of grace—working to complete man's natural desire of seeing God and of enjoying eternal happiness. No man can experience true joy without or outside of grace, for human life has no real duration if eternal life is not granted. Grace enables one to experience eternal life, which can begin in this life "through a mirror dimly" but will not be fulfilled until the complete glories of heaven (1 Cor 13:12).

There is perhaps no better way to introduce our subject on divine grace than to pray with the Church, whose liturgy contains inspired texts of praise and adoration, constituting an impressive compendium of doctrine and theology. On the sixteenth Sunday after Pentecost, the Church prays in the Collect: "May Thy grace, we beseech Thee, O Lord, ever go before us and follow us: and make us continually intent upon good works. Through our Lord Jesus Christ, Thy Son, Who with Thee liveth and reigneth in the unity of the Holy Ghost, God, world without end. Amen." Through the sacramental mediation of the priest, the faithful at Mass pray that God's grace may always be at their side, for without the workings of grace—both sanctifying and actual—we can do nothing (see Jn 15:5). In fact, the purpose of actual grace is always to help a person live in the state of habitual grace, which can be lost through mortal sin. Simply put, there is no Christian life without grace. Hence, all our preoccupation must tend towards safeguarding that divine life poured out upon us, and growing in it with the help of the theological and moral virtues, alongside the gifts of the Holy Spirit. What a treasure a soul possesses, to be in the state of grace, which builds within us a supernatural organism! On the other hand, what a horror to behold a soul in mortal sin, far, far away from home, as was the Prodigal Son (see Lk 15:11–31)!

As St. Thomas Aquinas says, grace produces faith— *gratia facit fidem*—and, alongside faith, hope and charity.

These virtues, termed the "theological virtues," are the highest Christian virtues, for they have God as their immediate and principal object, and accompany the infusion of sanctifying grace. This making of faith by grace is the process of justification, by which one passes from the state of sin to that of being a child of God through baptism. If perchance a soul has the misfortune to lose that initial sacramental infusion of sanctifying grace, he would lose charity as well. Faith, however, would still remain, though severely weakened and imperfect, for it no longer remains formed by charity.

It bears repeating: grace cannot exist without charity. If a soul has lost grace following the initial justification or sanctification in baptism, it can return to its former state by a sacramental confession, moved by that faith that yet remains in the soul. And alongside grace, charity returns as well. In any case, grace is the only means by which God gives us charity, thereby making us lovable—the charity by which God loves us and we, in turn, can love Him and our neighbor. Thus, there can be no love without the presence of grace. Of course, we are not speaking of God not loving us anymore, but in the sense that God is impeded in loving us, for in rejecting grace, we close ourselves to receiving His love. To reject His grace and to sin against Him is akin to building up a wall that prevents His love from reaching us. To return to our point, if we are not sanctified by grace and fail to *remain* in His love, we cannot share in the divine life, for grace makes one a partaker of the divine nature (see 2 Pt 1:4). Only by sanctifying grace and by living in grace can we really love God and our neighbor. Love without grace is not Christian charity but only a human sentiment. Hence, grace makes us capable of receiving God's love. Such grace is the prerequisite of the presence of love and love the expression of grace and its goal.

Grace and charity are tightly bound in an intimate relationship. We may observe this intimacy in the "wedding garment" of which St. Matthew's Gospel speaks (22:11). St. Gregory makes a beautiful comparison between this wedding garment and the virtue of charity, explaining that the one who is invited to the nuptial feast has faith, for otherwise he could not even enter into the wedding hall, but he lacks the charity enabling him to remain with the others. He states: "The marriage is the wedding of Christ and his church, and the garment is the virtue of charity: a person who goes into the feast without a wedding garment is someone who believes in the Church but does not have charity."[1] For St. Gregory, charity is rightly called the wedding garment, "for our Creator Himself wore the same garment when He came to the marriage with His Church." Therefore, all guests must attend the nuptials properly dressed. In fact, St. Gregory continues, "he comes without a wedding garment who does not safeguard within him the grace of charity."[2] Interestingly enough, we find here the intimate bond existing

---

[1] *In Evangelia Homiliae*, 36. For St. Jerome, "wedding garments are the Lord's commands and the works that are fulfilled from the Law and the Gospel." *Commentarius in Evangelium Matthaei*, III, 22.11–12.

[2] *In Evangelia Homiliae*, 36.

between grace and charity, to the point where they are either present together or concurrently non-existent.[3] Moreover, the "grace of charity" cannot be identified as an actual grace, allowing us to possess the virtue of charity, but rather it is the presence of sanctifying grace, which enriches the soul with that twofold charity towards God and neighbor. In other words, to have the "grace of charity" can only mean the possession of both grace and charity.

In fine, our present work aims principally at presenting the mystery of grace as the inner structure of theology, insofar as it opens up the understanding of Divine Revelation and enables us to live according to its demands. We will learn that divine grace is not something metaphorical, ethereal, or even hard to grasp (in a certain sense). On the contrary, grace is as real as our lives: it is the life of the soul and the bridge to the Mystery of God.

---

[3] For St. Thomas, these two are truly distinct, while for Blessed Duns Scotus, they are identical and only formally distinct.

1

Grace in Divine Revelation

THE MYSTERY OF DIVINE GRACE is revealed by God as the key aspect of Christian life. That God wanted to open up to mankind the mysteries of His inner life, to the extent of admitting all men of good will to be sharers in His divine life, speaks of the grandeur and centrality of divine grace in the Christian message. The Holy Scriptures together with Sacred Tradition are the sources from which we receive this important revelation. Let us now turn our gaze towards the Holy Scriptures, as they hand on to us the mystery of divine grace. After a scriptural overview, we will then focus our attention on what Sacred Tradition teaches us about grace. This will be the foundation stone for the theological comprehension of the mystery of grace we will develop in subsequent chapters.

The Mystery of Divine Grace in the Sacred Scriptures

1. *God's Grace in the Mystery of Creation*

To begin our study, we shall refer to the Old Testament as the remote preparation of Christian doctrine regarding the mystery of grace. Although these sacred texts do not mention a particular word designating the role of grace, we find elements that correspond, in a broader sense, to the idea of grace. "Grace" is first mentioned—although not by word—in the creation account. We do not see directly the concept of grace but rather a clear allusion to it. In this first "mentioning," we see creation marked by a distinctive freedom, bestowed as a gratuitous gift of God. The Creator, who, from the heavens, makes the world out of nothing, is at the same time keenly interested in the product of His hands, in the world and the creatures contained therein. God, accordingly, blesses this product of His condescension. For example, Adam and Eve are given the gift of freedom—the grace to choose to serve God or to follow their own appetites. As we know, they chose to follow the way of the flesh, and thus, lost the original graces and preternatural gifts bestowed on them by God. Thus, it is through Christ that we are made free and receive the grace to become God's children once again (Gal 5:1; Rom 8:17).

With the prophet Isaiah, we take an important step towards a deeper understanding of the mystery of grace. In his first song of the Servant of the Lord, the Lord speaks through the mouth of the servant, addressing first the people, then his suffering Son—"I have taken you by the hand and formed you; I have appointed you as covenant of the people and light of the nations" (Is 42:6).[4] From these

---

[4]   For the Biblical texts, we will normally make use of the translation offered by the Jerusalem Bible. When the translation is too far from the original, we will then refer to the Douay-Rheims translation.

words proceed all the Messianic works in which Christ is referred to as the Messiah of God in the New Testament (see Is 42:7 in relation to Mt 11:5 and Lk 4:18). Christ is the *covenant* for the people, and in this covenantal love, inaugurated by the Messiah, we will read the story of divine grace. Isaiah's announcement of the Servant of the Lord culminates in identifying the Creator with the Redeemer.

The prophet says: "Now thus says the Lord, who created you, Jacob, who formed you, Israel: do not be afraid, for I have redeemed you; I have called you by name, you are mine" (Is 43:1). Creation and redemption are two works of the same God. Creation is the beginning of all things, and redemption is a "new creation," in which the sin that damaged the original order is repaired, resulting in creation made anew in the blood of Christ. This will be the new beginning of creation, with a new life given to us—the life of grace. For this reason, St. Paul writes the following to the Corinthians: "For anyone who is in Christ, there is a new creation; the old creation has gone, and now the new one is here" (2 Cor 5:17). As we shall see, grace endows its recipient with this quality (among others): that of being created anew in Christ, in consequence of the Redemption. Even in the account of one of the greatest miracles of God, the passage of the Red Sea, creation and redemption are intimately bound up: God is the one who parts the seas, that all the redeemed might cross over (see Is 51:10).

God's Abode with Man

2. Grace under a Covenantal Form

The Covenant is at the very core of the Old Testament. The progressive revelation of God leads Him to establish with His people a pact of mutual relationship founded on the observance of the Law. In the covenant of Sinai, God gives this law to Moses, so that the Jewish nation might profess its faithfulness to YHWH. In turn, God assures them that their obedience to His voice would render them His property among the peoples of the earth (see Ex 19:5), "a kingdom of priests, a consecrated nation" (Ex 19:6). This covenant, especially with the prophets, will be laid out as a blessing upon the people, a way to be in a personal relationship with God. For instance, according to Isaiah (59:21), the covenant is to be endowed with God's spirit, so that the peoples might always retain His words in their mouths. According to Jeremiah (31:33), the Word of the Lord will be planted deep within all the peoples of Israel; it will be inscribed upon their hearts.

Moreover, it is important to keep in mind that, by the special covenant established already with Abraham under the form of a "blessing," all the peoples of the earth will be blessed. Abraham's obedience laid down an everlasting and universal blessing upon all the nations through his descendants (cf. Gen 22:16, 18). Here the catholicity, i.e., the universality, of God's promise is already perceptible.

All this brings into focus the *personal relationship* at the heart of the covenantal message: this relationship between God the Bridegroom and Israel the Bride, in which God loves His bride unfailingly, despite Israel's habitual infidelity to His eternal love. The Creator Himself has espoused Himself to Israel (see Jer 2:1; Is 43:4 and particularly 54:4–10). Moreover, this covenant will be characterized as a pact of love, foreshadowing the work and the presence of divine grace: a personal relationship with God, in His covenantal and perennial love. The words of the prophet Hosea resound with particular beauty: "I will betroth you to myself for ever, betroth you with integrity and justice, with tenderness and love" (Hos 2:21).

The Christian idea of grace is also prefigured in the Old Testament as a *forgiving love,* reestablishing man in a new condition. When God grants His forgiveness to sinners, their sins are wiped away, existing no more. Psalm 50 highlights the certain hope that God makes righteous the sinner, who can now stand before God's holiness: "O purify me, then I shall be clean; O wash me, I shall be whiter than snow. . . . A pure heart create for me, O God, put a steadfast spirit within me" (50:9, 12).

Ezekiel calls upon the power of God, that from on high He may pour forth His Spirit to breathe forth new life into "dry bones": "I am now going to make the breath enter you, and you will live. . . . I shall put my Spirit in you, and you will live" (37:5, 14), while Isaiah speaks of an outpouring of God's Spirit that shall turn the wilderness into a fertile land (32:15). Jeremiah clearly points out the forgiving mercy of God that makes man anew through a new "covenant," for the Law shall be written on the hearts of the people (31:33). Finally, it is Ezekiel again who announces the Lord's great promise to grant a new heart, intimately foreshadowing the new covenant He would lay down in the fullness of time: "I shall give you a new heart, and put a new spirit in you. I shall remove the heart of stone from you your bodies and give you a heart of flesh instead. I shall put my spirit in you, and make you keep my laws and sincerely respect my observances" (Ez 36:26–27). This "new heart" is a foreshadowing of the grace that will come through Christ and the New Covenant. Rather than relying on the old law of animal sacrifice, which only perpetuated the sins of the people, God will give mankind a "new spirit" of personal sacrifice, which may be fleshly (in the case of martyrdom), but is mostly spiritual.

3. Grace in the New Testament: A New Life in Christ

The New Testament is entirely permeated by the message of "grace" as the beginning of a new existence in Christ, who comes to redeem all mankind from sin. In Him, all prophecies are fulfilled. Indeed, God is among us to create a new heart for man: He Himself takes a heart of flesh, transforming that heart of stone into a fiery word of salvation. Behold how the economy of the Gospel of grace recapitulates the ancient law. These words from St. John's Gospel resound solemnly as a manifesto of Christian identity: "Indeed, from his fullness we have, all of us, received—yes, grace in return for grace, since, though the Law was given through Moses, grace and truth have come through Jesus Christ" (1:16–17).

Firstly, it is important to note that the word "grace" (*cháris* in Greek) in the New Testament does not always signify a supernatural gift that enables man to participate in God's nature, which is what we normally mean by it, and the meaning we will be discussing in these pages. Nor does the word "grace" always denote the supernatural order as such. It is St. Paul who principally uses this term in a strictly religious sense, which will gradually evolve into its present theological meaning. According to St. Paul's usage of this term, the doctrine of grace is built on a particular understanding of "supernatural grace," in the sense of a beginning of a new life, originating in the humanity of Christ, and diffusing over the entire world (see Col 1:6). We can even characterize the whole Pauline understanding of grace—which will have a particular influence over the entire New Testament understanding of grace—as "eternal life in Christ Jesus our Lord" (Rom 6:23). This, of course, does not exclude other meanings, but only delineates grace as a principle of new life as understood by St. Paul. This principle will consequently be brought forth into the Christian understanding as a key concept, on which all other New Testament features will focus. Grace as eternal life in our Lord is the quintessence of all expressions of the New Testament.[5]

3.1. Grace as a Gift of God

Grace is originally identified in the New Testament as a "divine gift." Although there are many graces and charisms (1 Cor 1:7; 12:4), they are all manifestations of one and the

---

[5]   Cf. Leo Scheffczyk, *Katholische Dogmatik* in *Die Heilsverwirkli-chung in der Gnade*, vol. 6 (Aachen: MM Verlag, 1998), 84.

same grace, which is the fundamental gift of God, transforming one's life, as it did St. Paul's. In fact, this zealous apostle of the Lord could glory in nothing but in the gift of grace, freely given and freely accepted from God (see 1 Cor 15:10; 2 Cor 1:12). Grace is salvation gained from God, in Christ, through faith, i.e., not by any action of man, but by a free gift from God, that no one may claim the credit (see Eph 2:8–9). Moreover, according to St. Paul, the gift of grace renders us righteous (see Rom 5:17), because it comes from Christ Himself: "... it is ever more certain that divine grace, coming through the one man, Jesus Christ, came to so many as an abundant free gift" (Rom 5:15). The terms "grace" and "charism" suggest the idea of gratuity, freely given with good will on the part of the giver.[6]

3.2. Grace as a New Life

This gift of God truly works a transformation of oneself, not only exteriorly, but principally interiorly—one that is deep and vital. St. Paul says that by the good act of one's man obedience, Christ Jesus "brings everyone life" (Rom 5:18). For this reason, he invites the Ephesians "to put on the new self that has been created in God's way, in the goodness and holiness of the truth" (4:24), and so to put aside the

---

[6]   In Greek, the two terms "grace" and "charism" have the same root: *cháris* and *chárisma*, deriving from the verb *charízomai*, which means, among other things, "to give graciously and generously." Johannes Louw and Eugene Nida, ed., *Greek-English Lexicon of the New Testament Based on Semantic Domains*, vol. 1: Introduction and Domains (New York: United Bible Societies, 1989), 583.

old self, corrupted by illusory desires. Salvation is a work of grace and grace brings man forth from the death of sin to a new life in Christ—to share, even here below, in the eternity of Christ. Essentially, we speak of an ontological transformation of one's entire being. We were dead, having sinned, but God so loved the world that he "brought us to life with Christ—it is through grace that you have been saved—and raised us up with him and gave us a place with him in heaven, in Christ Jesus" (Eph 2:5–6).

To be in Christ's grace, saved from eternal death and raised up in heaven, is indeed to be created by God in a new manner or, better yet, to be re-created. As St. Thomas Aquinas says in his commentary on 2 Cor 5:17, "The infusion of grace is a creation."[7] For this reason, theologians, in drawing from Divine Revelation all theological knowledge concerning the mystery of grace, will speak of grace as a "created" reality, to distinguish it from the "uncreated" grace, which is the Giver Himself, the Holy Spirit.[8] St. Thomas Aquinas comments:

> Hence he says, if anyone is in Christ, i.e., in the faith of Christ, or through Christ, he is a new creation [creature]: "For in Christ Jesus neither circumcision nor uncircumcision is of any avail, but faith working through love" (Gal 5:6). Here it should be noted that renewal by grace is called a creature. For creation is a

---

[7] St. Thomas Aquinas, *Commentary on the Second Epistle to the Corinthians*, 192.

[8] We will come back to this in the next chapter.

change from nothing to existence. But there are two kinds of existence, namely, of nature and of grace. The first creation was made when creatures were produced by God from nothing to exist in nature; and then the creature was new, but became old by sin: "He has made my flesh and my skin waste away" (Lam 3:4). Therefore, a new creation was required by which we would be produced to exist in grace. This, too, is a creation from nothing because those who lack grace are nothing: "And if I understand all mysteries and all knowledge, and if I have all faith, so as to remove mountains, but have not love, I am nothing" (1 Cor 13:2); "In his tent," i.e., of sin, "dwells that which is none of his" (Job 18:15). Augustine says: "For sin is nothing, and men become nothing when they sin." So it is clear that the infusion of grace is a creation.[9]

It is chiefly St. John the Evangelist who speaks of grace as a new life in Christ. Perhaps he himself heard the words spoken to Nicodemus: "I tell you solemnly, unless a man is born through water and the Spirit, he cannot enter the kingdom of God" (Jn 3:5). Here, the Master refers to the necessity of baptism to enter into the kingdom of heaven, that sacrament of Christian initiation enabling man to be reborn in grace. In fact, man needs to be "born from above" (Jn 3:3) by the Holy Spirit. Being reborn in this way happens

---

[9]   St. Thomas Aquinas, *Commentary on the Second Epistle to the Corinthians*, 192.

by "water and the Spirit," of which our Lord commands His apostles: "All authority in heaven and on earth has been given to me. Go, therefore, make disciples of all the nations; baptize them in the name of the Father and the Son and of the Holy Spirit . . ." (Mt 28:18–19).

Already in the prologue to his Gospel, St. John elucidates that the newly baptized are reborn "not out of human stock or urge of the flesh or will of man, but of God himself" (Jn 1:13). Thus, Christian life, this new life in Christ, is not a way to practice religion on the natural plane, but rather a way to share in Christ's own life, to be generated *into* and *through* this new generation of the Word of God made flesh (see Jn 1:14). Christ is the firstborn of many brothers, not in the flesh, but in the spirit through baptism (see Rm 8:29). To those who accepted and believed in Him "he gave the power to become children of God" (Jn 1:12). In baptism, man is configured to Christ, sharing in His eternal life, thus possessing eternal life. Those who are reborn through this wondrous sacrament carry about themselves the "image" of Christ—they are generated as children of God in the Son by faith, and so loved by the Father and sanctified by the Holy Spirit. Let us examine this more in depth.

This beautiful mystery of our regeneration in Christ is synthesized by St. Peter in a way that truly expresses the mystery of divine grace: we are made capable, by the power of God, "of sharing the divine nature" (see 2 Pt 1:4). Therefore, grace enables us to be partakers of the very life of God: this new life received in baptism is a participation in God's divine nature. Between Christ and a creature reborn in Him, there exists a "bond" of intimate unity, which strengthens the whole mystical body, the Church. This bond of deep and supernatural unity is sanctifying grace, as expressed by St. John in the parable of the vine and the branches (see Jn 15:1–17). Christ is the true vine, and all His disciples, generated by His grace, are the branches. As branches grafted into the vine bring forth fruit, sharing in the same life circulating therein, the same disciples, made one with Christ, must remain in Him to bear fruit. This figure of the vine illustrates well the supernatural life of grace circulating in the mystical organism: both in the Church and in each baptized soul remaining in Christ, being made one with Him in grace, or, as St. John says, by remaining in His love (see Jn 15:9). Here we see that the life of the vine—the grace of the Lord—is also the love of the Lord. Remaining in Christ means remaining in His love. Thus, grace and love are intimately united.

St. Paul expresses the same doctrine of the unity between Christ and His disciples with the image of the body and its members (see 1 Cor 12:12–27). As a collection of body parts, many though they be, are united and become "one," vivified by the same circulation of life, likewise with Christ and His mystical body. Of this mystical body, we form the various members, animated by the Spirit present within us—the Spirit of the Lord. By this participation in the divine life by supernatural generation in the Holy Spirit, we are indeed children of God and the Holy Spirit bears witness to it (see Rom 8:16). Therefore, grace, as new life poured forth within us, introduces us into new relations with God—that of divine filiation with the Father in Christ, by the Holy Spirit. The Holy Trinity abides within those regenerated by grace as sharers of the divine nature. It is by grace—and only by grace—that we can truly address God as Our Father who is in heaven.

3.3. Grace as the Presence of the Holy Trinity

Both St. John and St. Paul, the preeminent instructors of the mystery of grace, prefer to present this mystery as the operative presence of the Holy Trinity within the soul. This is a great mystery. In order to enlighten its depths, we may begin at the moment of the Annunciation when the Angel addresses our Lady as "full of grace." The Angel immediately adds the following words: "the Lord is with thee" (Lk 1:28). Grace is then the presence of the Lord in our Lady's soul. For that reason, her soul magnifies the Lord (see Lk 1:46); for in her, God Himself is present—God who takes flesh within her. And wherever God is present, there likewise is the Holy Trinity.

This new life present in the man reborn in grace is expressed by Christ in His final discourse before entering His passion. Speaking to His disciples, the Lord said: "If anyone loves me he will keep my word, and my Father will love him, and we shall come to him and make our home with him" (Jn 14:23). This is the doctrine of the inhabitation of the Holy Trinity residing in the soul of one who loves the Lord, in the one who remains faithful to this love. God the Holy Trinity abides in a person who possesses this new life within him. More precisely, this new life is the operation of the mystery of the Most Holy Trinity within the depths of the soul in grace. Grace renders souls capable of participating in the intimate life of God, in those divine processions in which the Father generates the Son, and the Father and the Son breathe forth the Holy Spirit. Though incapable by natural means, the soul is capable of sharing in the inner life of God by the divine bond infused into the soul. Thus, grace sanctifies the soul transformed into the dwelling of the Most High.

St. Paul also describes man's regeneration as a conse-cration of his whole body in consequence of the special inhabitation of the Holy Spirit. Man is God's temple and the Spirit of God is the living presence abiding in this bodily temple. If a man perchance destroys this presence by losing God's grace—such as through mortal sin—God will destroy him (see 1 Cor 3:16), in the sense that, as St. Thomas Aquinas says, man without grace is nothing; he is annihilated or brought back into his nothingness. Con-trariwise, a person in grace truly builds up within himself the temple of God, and must act accordingly by keeping holy the temple of his body (see 1 Cor 6:19–20).

To summarize, we can say that grace, in the New Tes-tament, shines forth clearly as the fruit of Redemption, brought about by Christ as a new life given to those who submit to His divine majesty. This fruit, coming forth from the tree of life, the holy Cross, works a perfect interior and integral justice in those who, through faith and love, obey Christ (see Mk 1:15; 16:16; Mt 10:32–39). This is the justice or sanctity given back to man after its loss by original and actual sin. God justifies us or sanctifies us, not by disregarding our condition as sinners, but by giving us the Spirit of His Son, who works out this new and eternal generation in the likeness of Christ (see Rom 8:10–11). This spirit of Christ, the Holy Spirit, makes us children of God and coheirs with Christ (see Rom 8:17). Dwelling in the soul regenerated by grace, the soul becomes a temple of the Holy Trinity, thus building up in this world the true Temple, the Church of Christ.

The Mystery of Divine Grace
in the Fathers of the Church

1. Grace in the Greek Fathers

The Sacred Scriptures have depicted a beautiful sketch of the mystery of grace, described especially by St. John the Evangelist and St. Paul. The Fathers of the Church, succeeding the apostles, have deepened this doctrine and have the great merit of systematizing it, laying out precisely its features and distinctions. The first ones to discuss this doctrine were the Greek Fathers. They contemplated above all the moment of man's elevation to the supernatural order in relation to the original fall of Adam and Eve. Man was elevated in grace, but because of the sin of disobedience, he lost this gift, and his nature was wounded by original sin. Christ with His Redemption freed mankind from sin, so that those who welcome His grace are brought back to that original condition in which sin is destroyed, enabling man to contemplate God once again.

God's Abode with Man

For the Eastern Fathers, St. Peter's text (2 Pt 1:4) was a guide to comprehending the activity of grace. In their understanding, grace enabled man to share in God's own nature, to be, to a certain extent, deified so as to be as intimate with Him as the Son is with the Father. In fact, man *is* partaker of the divine nature. In harmony with Greek philosophical thought and with the support of the book of Wisdom, the Greek Fathers understood the work of divine grace as the divinization of man, making man participant in two divine attributes: immortality (*athanasía*) and incorruptibility (*aphtharsía*). Only God is incorruptible by nature for He is not generated (*agénnetos*); man can be so only by participation through grace. This plan of restored and incorruptible life is brought forward by God in three stages: a) Adam's elevation in grace; b) Adam's sin, and consequently the loss of all supernatural gifts; and c) the restoration of man's primitive condition by the work of the Word incarnate.

The work of Redemption is a recapitulation and a reinstatement of mankind in Christ, which is the aim of the doctrine of "divinization" or "deification" (*theopoieîn*). Christ is the new Adam and Adam's offspring is made anew in Him. The biblical texts that support this doctrine reduce to the following: "Let us make man in our own image, in the likeness of ourselves . . ." (Gen 1:26); "I have said to you: 'You are gods and all of you, sons of the Most High" (Ps 81:6); and ". . . to share the divine nature and to escape corruption in a world that is sunk in vice" (2 Pt 1:4).

The first to use the technical term "divinization" was St. Clement of Alexandria: "With his celestial doctrine (the Logos) deifies man."[10] But St. Athanasius properly illustrates the mind of the Greek Fathers, characterized by the idea of participation in the divine nature, of re-birth through the divine Spirit, and of adoption as sons to be created anew in Christ, a preeminent concept in the theological idea of *theopoíesis* (deification):[11] "The Son of God became Son of man so that the sons of men, that is, of Adam, might become sons of God . . . partakers of the life of God. . . . Thus He is Son of God by nature, and we by grace."[12] The very goal of Christ's Redemption is the deification or divine filiation (*uiopoieîn*) of man. St. Cyril of Alexandria makes the same point: "We are made partakers of the divine nature and are said to be sons of God, nay we are actually called divine, not only because we are exalted by grace to supernatural glory, but also because we have God dwelling in us."[13] Through baptism, grace is imparted to our souls, and in this way, we share the divine life of God, because we are no longer enslaved to sin but are free in the grace of Christ. Next, the Holy Eucharist brings this deification to completion, especially for the body, because the Savior is truly within us—indeed,

---

[10] St. Cyril of Alexandria, *Paedagogus*, 1.12, Patrologiae Cursus Completus, Series Graeca, ed. Jacques-Paul Migne, vol. 9 (Paris: 1857–1866), col. 413 (hereafter, PG).

[11] Cf. John Norman Davidson Kelly, *Early Christian Doctrines* (London: Adam & Charles Black, 1958), 352.

[12] St. Athanasius, *De Incarnatione* 54.7, PG 25:192.

[13] St. Cyril of Alexandria, *In Iohannis Evangelium* 1.9, PG 73:157.

He dwells within us.[14] St. Cyril compares—with due differences—the union between the Eucharistic Lord and the communicant with the union of the divine Word and His human nature. The Holy Spirit assists in helping us to become conformed to the Son of God and realizes in us the inhabitation of the Triune God; He imprints on us the seal of the Holy Trinity.[15]

This great oriental inheritance was taken up later by St. John Damascene, who follows in the same footsteps. He distinguishes more clearly between the divinization of nature and that of the person: the former happening at the moment of the Incarnation by contact with the divinity of the Logos,[16] the latter happening subordinately to the human effort to cooperate with God in the imitation of Christ and in making use of the sacraments of the Church.

2. Grace in the Western Church. St. Augustine and the Problem of Pelagius

In the Western Church, St. Augustine wrote extensively on the doctrine of grace, and has thus been given the name, "Doctor of Grace." In his writings, the theology of grace witnessed a great moment of systematization regarding significant theological topics, such as predestination to

---

[14] St. Cyril of Alexandria, *In Iohannis Evangelium* 6.54, PG 73:572–80.

[15] St. Cyril of Alexandria, *In Isaiam* 44.21–22, PG 70:936.

[16] St. John Damascene, *De imagine*, 1.21, PG 94:1253.

salvation, the concourse of free will with grace, sufficient grace, and efficacious grace, among many others. All subsequent developments of grace throughout the ages begin with an interpretation of the Doctor of Hippo—such was his influence on our understanding of this mystery.

The providential occasion for deepening the mystery of grace, for articulating its beauty and necessity, was offered to St. Augustine by Pelagius, a British monk, who set out for Africa to escape the invasion of Alaric, eventually fleeing to Rome, where he established himself. Pelagius was quite circumspect, for only a few could read his writings, none of which were signed by the author himself.[17] His doctrine can be summarized in a few points:

1. Adam was created mortal, independently from his sin;

2. Rather than affecting the entire human race, Adam's sin damaged only himself. Moreover, as his sin did not affect the entirety of mankind but only himself, Christ did not raise up all of mankind in his resurrection;

3. All babies are born in Adam's state prior to original sin—that is, original justice—and consequently do not need baptism to gain salvation and eternal life;

---

[17] Pelagius's major work is called *Testimonies*, a collection of biblical citations, whose existence is attested and critically analyzed by St. Jerome in the *Dialogus*, I.25–30, and by St. Augustine in *De natura et gratia*.

4. Baptism, therefore, is not absolutely necessary for obtaining eternal life, but only for entering the kingdom of heaven (which, in his opinion, is the Church);

5. Since man is not born in original sin, the fundamental principle of the moral life is the omnipotence of free will. For Pelagius, man can always, and because of his natural strength, do good.

6. The assumption that man could not help sinning was seen by the British monk as an insult to the Creator. St. Augustine's prayer: "Give what thou commandest, and command what thou wilt,"[18] distressed Pelagius particularly, for it seemed to suggest that men were only puppets determined by the movement of divine grace. For Pelagius, man was free, out of his own capability. He was the owner of an unconditional free will and responsibility.[19]

---

[18] St. Augustine, *Confessiones*, 10, 40. The figure of Pelagius became prominent because of his dispute with St. Jerome, criticizing his ascetical teaching about marriage. Studying more accurately the source of St. Jerome that recounts Pelagius's thoughts, a revised perspective of the figure of this British monk might emerge. See Robert F. Evans, *Pelagius: Inquiries and Reappraisals* (New York: The Seabury Press, 1968). For more extensive information on Pelagianism, see John Ferguson, *Pelagius: A Historical and Theological Study* (Cambridge: W. Heffer & Sons, 1956), 159–85.

[19] Kelly, *Early Christian Doctrines*, 357.

St. Augustine realized immediately the enormous danger of these theses, which logically concluded in a radical denial of Christ's Redemption, starting from a natural understanding of the supernatural order—one in which divine grace had no significant role to play. Pelagius's teachings mark the beginning of "naturalism." Because Pelagius argues against original sin, this means that grace is no longer necessary.

St. Augustine's exegesis of the Letter to the Romans draws out the major points of his response to Pelagius, in order to reject his heretical assumptions, even if he does seem to exaggerate. Sometimes exaggeration is necessary to emphasize the opposite view, in order to make clear the exact nature of the truth. Pelagius would later be solemnly condemned during the Council of Carthage (418), which promulgated the true doctrine of grace in nine points. Pope Zosimus also confirmed the authentic doctrine of grace in the document *Epistula tractoria*,[20] in which he expressed his admiration for the great zeal and work of the African bishops.

Augustine is firmly convinced of the existence of original sin. Aside from Genesis, he finds Scriptural proofs in Psalm 50, Job, and Ephesians 2:3[21] and—as already mentioned—especially in Romans 5:12 and John 3:3–5.

---

[20] *Scriptorum Ecclesiasticorum*, Patrologiae Cursus Completus, Series Latina, ed. Jacques-Paul Migne, vol. 20 (Paris 1857–1866), coll. 693–95 (hereafter, PL).

[21] *Enarrationes in Psalmos* 50, 10 and *Sermo* 170, 2.

Before engaging in this dispute with Pelagius, the Holy Doctor of Hippo had already clarified that the freedom man possessed before original sin had to be understood not in the sense of inability to sin (the *non posse peccare*, which is the true liberty enjoyed only in heaven), but in the sense of ability not to sin (*posse non peccare*).[22] As a consequence of our loss of original grace in Adam's sin, we have lost, with Adam, the liberty not to sin (*libertas*). Henceforth, we cannot avoid sin without God's grace, and still more, without a special grace, we are unable to do good. Grace is therefore necessary to choose the good and to avoid sin, although man still retains, after original sin, his free will (*liberum arbitrium*).

The Augustinian distinction between *liberty* (the ability to choose good)[23] and *free will* (the possibility to choose between good and evil, notwithstanding man's tendency to immoral and even perverse choices), is truly fundamental. There is no opposition between grace and free will; on the contrary, it is grace that confers freedom and enables man to overcome temptations. With grace, man is free to live a true life, the life God desires of him.[24]

---

[22] *De correptione et gratia*, 33.

[23] Enjoyed by the Blessed Virgin Mary as Immaculate Conception (no concupiscence or disorder was present in her) and by the Saints in heaven.

[24] *Opus imperfectum contra Iulianum*, 6.11. In this work *Against Julian*, who held that freedom was nothing else than the capacity of man to choose voluntarily good and evil, so as to deny that freedom is for good whereas free will the capacity to choose

Although Augustine's doctrine on grace met with increasing overall consent, certain monks in southern France —such as St. John Cassian and St. Vincent of Lérins—were unhappy with his theory on grace and free will. It was St. Faustus of Riez who wrote the treatise *De Gratia* on behalf of these bishops. The treatise took a more naturalistic tone than Cassian's opinions on the matter. Granted, they advocated for the necessity of grace for one's salvation, since they believed in original sin, and for God's aid concurring with man's free will; however, the French monks believed that man, too, should be able to make decisions himself regarding his eternal destiny. Thus, they postulated in particular that the "beginning of faith" (*initium fidei*), as described by St. John Cassian, and the "feeling of credulity" (*credulitatis affectus*) as described by St. Faustus, depended on man's free choice. Freedom would precede grace only in the initial

---

also evil, St. Augustine replies that if this were freedom, God would not be free. But man's Redemption is for the freedom of eternal beatitude even though, out of free will, man could reject it. Here is the original Augustinian text: "Redimuntur ergo, quicumque redimuntur, ab eo qui venit quaerere quod perierat, qui et antequam in carne veniret, per fidem ipsam redemit, qua credebatur esse venturus. Redimuntur autem in libertatem beatitudinis sempiternam, ubi iam peccato servire non possint. Nam si, ut dicis, boni malique voluntarii possibilitas sola libertas est, non habet libertatem Deus, in quo peccandi possibilitas non est. Hominis vero liberum arbitrium congenitum et omnino inamissibile si quaerimus, illud est quo beati omnes esse volunt, etiam hi qui ea nolunt quae ad beatitudinem ducunt."

decision to believe, while it would concur the moment the free decision was made.

As with Pelagianism, St. Augustine rose up against this position, which he saw as a tempered threat to the precedence and absolute necessity of grace, and wrote one of his masterpieces, *De praedestinatione Sanctorum* (*The Predestination of Saints*). Grace and freedom, for the Bishop of Hippo, are never concurrent: freedom is an effect of grace, for "where the Spirit of the Lord is, there is freedom" (2 Cor 3:17). The will is not annulled, but it can truly be free and delivered from evil only when vivified by grace. This concept was greatly expanded in order to address another issue, one not exempt from additional problems—that of the eternal predestination of man either to salvation or to final condemnation. We will deal with this topic in the next chapter.

So far, it is already worth noticing that, for St. Augustine, the whole of mankind constitutes a *massa damnata*—a universal mass of perdition,[25] destined to everlasting damnation were it not for the grace of the Redemption of Christ. Even children dying without the grace of baptism are, for Augustine, destined to eternal fire in hell with the devil, although their sufferings will be mild as compared to those who willingly committed sins.[26]

---

[25] *Ad Simplicianum*, I, 2, 16: I, 2, 20. *De gratia Christi et de peccato originali*, 2, 34.

[26] *Sermo* 294, 2–4, *De Baptismo parvulorum contra Pelagianos*. Cf. Kelly, *Early Christian Doctrine*, 362–66. From this position, little by little, emerged the mild doctrine of limbo, i.e., that babies

Thus was the Augustinian doctrine on grace extensively laid down. The subsequent development will always return to it as an unavoidable reference.[27]

---

who die without the sacrament of baptism experience natural happiness, without enjoying the Beatific Vision.

[27] Cf. Kelly, *Early Christian Doctrine*, 362–66.

2

God the Giver and Grace as a Divine Gift

IN THIS CHAPTER, we will first focus on God as the giver of all that is good: everything that is perfect is given us from above, from the Father of all light (see Jas 1:17). God is the giver of grace, disposed from all eternity in His salvific plan of salvation, which is indeed a salvific plan of grace. Grace was foreseen (*praevisa*—related to the notion of predestination) as a means to eternal happiness for all humans even before the first sin of Adam. In fact, even before the world was made, God chose us in Christ to be holy and spotless in His presence in charity (see Eph 1:4). First comes love, and, as we will come to see, God is always first with His inscrutable but salvific will: a will of love. I will be discussing the topic of predestination in this chapter, in order to examine the relationship between God's grace and man's free will, which is never undermined but only strengthened and elevated by that grace.

The Universal Salvific Will of God

As St. Paul writes to Timothy, God our Savior "wants everyone to be saved and reach full knowledge of the truth" (1 Tim

2:4). It is worth noting that this salvation, which God desires for all, is intimately bound up with the truth. Humans can be saved if they adhere to the truth, with their consciences open to the moral good, namely, open to God, and then to Christ, who is the truth, the way, and the life (see Jn 14:6). Truth is ultimately Christ, in His person and in His doctrine of salvation.[28] Truth leads always to Him, and only to Him. Hence, God's desire of salvation for all means an invitation to all men of good will to receive and live by the gift of divine grace, which is the only means to our supernatural end.

Grace, therefore, precedes man's decision and opens up a pathway towards eternal salvation. Insofar as all men are capable of knowing the truth, they too are capable of finding salvation in God through His grace. Thus, we come easily from the natural order of creation to the supernatural order of salvation. These two orders are not mutually exclusive but require one other in the order of time, because the natural order must be elevated by the supernatural in order to be redeemed in Christ. Furthermore, there is no possibility of having salvific grace if there is no human nature to elevate to a supernatural state; conversely, there is no eternal salvation for man outside of the grace of Christ. Here we have an initial sketch of the relationship between nature and grace, a topic we shall tackle in the fourth chapter.

---

[28] 1 Tim 2:4 says that God wants salvation for those who come to know the truth, or *epígnosin aletheías* (cf. Heb 10:26). This "has become a technical form for the intellectual acceptance of Christianity." Walter Lock, *A Critical and Exegetical Commentary on the Pastoral Epistles* (Edinburgh: T&T Clark, 1936), 27.

Let us now turn back to the mystery of God's universal salvific will. Why is it so preponderant in every discourse about grace? In the words of the German theologian, Michael Schmaus,

> God's salvific will leaves no one out, it is directed towards every individual. The universality of God's salvific will coincides with the universality of his redemptive will. The testimony of Scripture to the universal efficacy of Jesus Christ's life and saving actions and to Jesus' meaning for all men coincides with the testimony to the universal salvific will. God's universal salvific will has its foundation in that love which led him at the beginning to create a realm of reality distinct from himself.[29]

Once again, this highlights the strong bond existing between creation and salvation. The universality of God's salvific will lies ultimately in this unshakable foundation of God's free love, poured out upon creation out of nothing. According to Schmaus, it would have been a great contradiction if God, rather than desiring the eternal well-being of all creatures, had desired their eternal misfortune, after having shown such great love in creating them for no other reason than His gratuitous love.[30] This indeed would cause dismay, and would depict only an egoistic behavior, unbecoming of God.

---

[29] Michael Schmaus, *Dogma: Justification and the Last Things*, vol. 6 (London: Sheed and Ward, 1977), 3.

[30] Cf. Schmaus, *Dogma*, 3–4.

However, it must also be considered that, if God's salvific will is directed towards everyone, without compelling anyone but respecting human freedom, salvation itself is not a necessity but a gift. Because it is a gift from God, it may also be rejected by one's freedom. God never imposes salvation upon anyone, but rather, He asks for human cooperation. Of course, grace can never fail in and of itself, because God can never be deceived by man or simply make His right judgement after a person makes his or her own decision; grace always and necessarily accomplishes its end, because it does not require human action for its completion. On the other hand, man's freedom is not a joke or fake and for this reason, one is able to refuse salvation. The Holy Scriptures do not unveil the mysterious encounter of God's call and man's response. Rather, we see ourselves in the presence of a tremendous mystery. Because of its challenging nature, it opened up one of the most passionate disputes among theologians, starting with the considerations of St. Augustine.

Predestination as Choice and Love Ahead of Time

A premise here is due: with this challenging topic of predestination, we come to know, once again, the intimate link between the order of creation and that of salvation—orders that have their origin in God's eternity with His "divine plan." The first stage of this plan, according to the Letter of St. Paul to the Romans (8:29), is thus described: "For those whom he foreknew he also predestined." There are two verbs to dwell upon here. The first is "foreknew"—to know ahead of time, which in Greek is rendered with *pro-égno* (from *pró-ginósko*), and can be translated as either "to know" or "to choose" ahead of time. Here the idea of freely creating all things out of pure love returns. God foreknew and foreloved those whom He created. It is His knowledge and His love that call all things into being, some of which are made to exist in His image and likeness (see Gen 1:26). Henceforth, creation is the foundation for justification and glorification (see Rom 8:30). As O'Callaghan comments: "We can see that the work of creation is the basis or foundation of the entire divine design or plan. On the basis of what God created, God acts, chooses, calls, justifies, prepares humanity for the eternal marriage feast."[31]

The other verb to consider is "predestined," which in Greek is *proórisen*—pre-determine, i.e., to determine before or to ordain. Those who are predestined are those who have been foreknown or chosen before. What does "before" here properly mean? This text from Romans helps us to understand another Pauline text, which describes the order of this predestination:

> Before the world was made, he (God the Father) chose us, chose us in Christ, to be holy and spotless, and to live through love in his presence. He predestined us in love to be his sons through Jesus Christ, according to the purpose of his will, to the praise of

---

[31] Paul O'Callaghan, *God Ahead of Us: The Story of Divine Grace* (Minneapolis: Fortress Press, 2014), 16.

his glorious grace which he freely bestowed on us
in the Beloved. (Eph 1:4–6)

This text demonstrates that we have been chosen collectively
in Christ to be holy in His presence. But the "first born of all
creation" (Col 1:15) is Christ, who "was predestined before
the foundation of the world but was made manifest at the
end of the times for your sake" (1 Pet 1:20). In Him, God
predestined the whole human race, even though each person
must choose to follow Christ of his own accord. Therefore,
the first principle is that there is no predestination outside of
Christ or without Christ. He is the one who has been predestined and is the reason for the predestination of all others.
This reality will enlighten an accurate understanding of the
mystery of individual predestination. This issue has arisen over
the past centuries as one of the most problematic theological
issues. The text to the Ephesians speaks of "us" in the plural,
meaning the Church as a whole body of believers. But what
about each and every individual? The aforementioned text to
the Colossians might already offer us an answer: since Christ
is *the predestined*, only those *in Christ* are consequently predestined, those who were foreknown and foreloved in Him
and have conformed their lives to Him, *remaining in Him*.

1. Predestination as Understood by Theologians
over the Centuries

Undoubtedly, St. Augustine's position is central to the comprehension of the idea of a personal predestination. Let us
bear in mind that predestination is eternal, outside of time, and

foreseen in the unique plan of salvation, which God worked out in Christ. But what does it mean that God predestines an individual person to glory? Does this imply that someone else is not predestined? But, if this were the case, why might a person *not* be predestined to glory and therefore condemned to eternal dismay? The proper explanation to these questions lies in a correct understanding of the relationship between grace and free will.

On the one hand, according to St. Augustine, God's omnipotent will, operating on our will by grace, is irresistible. God can never fail in giving His grace. On the other hand, St. Augustine acknowledges that God works through our own will, so that the effects of grace depend also on our spontaneous and free response and cooperation.[32] It is also true that God in His foreknowledge (*praescientia*) sees from eternity man's response to His grace and acts accordingly, predisposing all in order to respect that choice.

However, St. Augustine pushes himself further on this issue, when he stresses more the precedence of grace in relation to the whole of mankind, that—as we already said—is a *massa damnata*. Grace takes always the initiative; since men are already condemned, being born in original sin, it is always an "unmerited grace" to be accepted, but it is God who determines who shall receive grace and who shall not. For St. Augustine, the number of the elect is limited, corresponding to the number of fallen angels to be replaced.[33]

---

[32] St. Augustine, *De correptione et gratia*, 45.
[33] *De civitate Dei*, 22.I.2.

In so doing, the Bishop of Hippo had to twist the New Testament text, which speaks about God's universal will of salvation (1 Tim 2:4). For St. Augustine, this text means that God wills the salvation of all the *elect*. God, then, has mercy on those whom He wishes to justify, and hardens those upon whom he does not wish to bestow His mercy. It is not a divine caprice, or a purely arbitrary choice, because no one is entitled to salvation before God, all being enslaved by Satan and sin.[34] Predestination, for St. Augustine, is a foreknowledge and a divine favor "to infallibly deliver those who will be delivered."[35] Here, rather than clarifying the mystery, arises a new issue: how can God decide whom he shall liberate? Does this not lead, in the end, to an arbitrary decision or even to predestining some to eternal condemnation?

In fact, in the ninth century, there was a great controversy over the concept of "double predestination," in which, it is argued, some are chosen for glory and others for eternal damnation. As Brian Matz argues, it is only St. Isidore of Seville who uses this term in his *Sententiae* II.6, which is, in fact, a condensed version of passages

---

[34] Cf. Kelly, *Early Christian Doctrine*, 367–69.

[35] *De dono perseverantia*, 14, 35. This work is also known as the second book of the *Praedestinatio Sanctorum*. The full Latin text reads: "Haec est praedestinatio sanctorum, nihil aliud: praescientia scilicet, et praeparatio beneficiorum Dei, quibus certissime liberantur, quicumque liberantur." The English text reads: "This is the predestination of the saints — nothing else; to wit, the foreknowledge and the preparation of God's kindnesses, whereby they are most certainly delivered, whoever they are that are delivered."

from St. Gregory the Great's *Moralia in Iob*.[36] Thus, when
Gottschalk of Orbais (c. 808–c. 868) and Ratramnus of
Corbie make arguments for this theory, they are taking their positions not from St. Augustine but from St.
Isidore. As Matz explains, "The double predestinarians
took Isidore's 'Gregory-inspired' language in *Sententiae*
II.6 and made it the primary lens through which they
read Augustine, Gregory, the scriptures, and almost every
other source to which they turned for support. Isidore is
the source of an explicit double predestination."[37] In 853,
a synod was convoked in Quierzy (France) and rejected
this position in the following manner:

> The omnipotent God wishes "all men" without ex-
> ception "to be saved" (1 Tim 2:4), even if not all are
> saved. That some, however, are saved is the gift of
> the one who saves; that some, however, perish is the
> fault of those who perish. Just as there is not, nor
> has been, nor will be any man whose nature has not
> been assumed by Christ Jesus our Lord, so also there
> is not, nor has been, nor will be any man for whom
> he has not suffered, even if not all are redeemed by
> the mystery of his Passion. That not all, however, are

---

[36] Brian J. Matz, "Augustine in the Predestination Controversy of
the Ninth Century, Part I: The Double Predestinarians Gottschalk of Orbais and Ratramnus of Corbie," *Augustinian Studies*
46.2 (2015): 176–77. *Isidorus Hispalensis Sententiae*, ed. Pierre
Cazier, CCSL 111:103, II.6.

[37] Matz, "Augustine in the Predestination Controversy," 177.

redeemed by the mystery of his Passion concerns neither the greatness nor the fullness of the price, but, rather, the part of those who are unfaithful and those who do not believe with the faith "which works through love" (Gal 5:6).[38]

This condemnation of Gottschalk clarified the proper way to understand predestination: God wishes for all men to be saved, even if not all are saved. The fact that some men are not saved is due to their choice to live against God's commandments.

Unfortunately, the incorrect doctrine of double predestination was assumed by Martin Luther and especially by John Calvin. In his *Institutes*, Calvin affirms that just as some are predestined to heaven, so are others predestined to hell; God Himself *drives* them to hell, and they cannot escape it.[39] Luther had affirmed almost the same. According to him, God saves or damns those whom he wishes. The only way to affirm God's omnipotence definitively is to uphold God's sovereign *arbitrium*. God, for Luther, is an arbitrary judge.

---

[38] DH 623–24.

[39] Calvin reinforced his view about the predestination of the elect to glory and of the wicked to eternal dismay by arguing that the hardening of the hearts of the non-elect is as much attributable to God as is mercy. Cf. John Calvin, *Institutes of the Christian Religion*, vol. III, cc. 21–23, ed. John T. McNeill, *The Library of Christian Classics*, vol. I (London: Westminster Press, 1960). See also Charles Journet, *The Meaning of Grace* (London: Geoffrey Chapman, 1960), 50.

The topic of predestination is truly challenging. Can we at this stage clearly explain this mystery? First, it is important to remember that the word "predestination" is a construction, with the prefix *pre*, which signifies priority, not of time but of dignity and excellence. If this anteriority were chronological, it would be easy to conclude that everything was a prewritten scenario planned out by God. On the contrary, if anyone is not predestined it is only because he refuses the call.[40] In God we can distinguish between a twofold knowledge: a) a *scientia antecedens*—a knowledge that precedes human decision and b) a *scientia consequens*—a knowledge that follows it, since God knows everything with one pure act of intellect from all eternity.

Besides this twofold knowledge, theologians have also distinguished a twofold grace: *gratia sufficiens* (sufficient grace) and *gratia efficax* (efficacious grace). The former might fail to bring about salvation because of man's abuse of freedom, while the latter can never fail and produces always what it means, that is, eternal salvation. It is St. Augustine who *in primis* speaks of an "invincible grace" (*gratia invicta*),[41] of which Holy Scripture points out its irresistible nature in being "imposed" upon men (see Ezek 36:27; Rom 9:19; 1 Cor 15:10; Phil 2:13). But there are also other Scriptural passages that speak of a sufficient grace which humans can resist by opposing their wills to it (see Isa 5:4; Acts 7:51; Mt 23:37).

---

40   Cf. Journet, *Meaning of Grace*, 47–48.
41   St. Augustine, *De correptione et gratia*, 12, 38.

God does not decide to predestine certain souls to eternal damnation, although He already knows those who will refuse His call to salvation. His knowledge that follows man's choice does not influence it, but rather safeguards its wholly human and free aspect. Hence, we can say with Cardinal Journet that "God abandons and rejects those who, as he *sees, from all eternity*, take the first initiative in the final refusal of his prevenient grace."[42] In Christ all have been predestined to salvation, and everyone has been given the sufficient grace to be saved. Those who remain faithful to Christ are saved and bring to completion the sufficient grace they have been given. Those who are lost forever are those who have freely rejected God's sufficient grace and have relied on their frail wills. Ultimately, predestination belongs to the mystery of God, and for us mortals, is always quite challenging and impenetrable. Its mystery remains hidden from men.[43]

2. The Dispute "De Auxiliis" concerning the Activity of Grace and Free Will

The theological debates regarding the mystery of predestination continued into the period following the Council of Trent, particularly regarding the aid of grace to free will—called *de auxiliis*. Related to our topic is the idea that predestination to salvation is offered as an efficacious

---

[42] Journet, *Meaning of Grace*, 50.

[43] See Council of Trent, *Decree on Justification*: DH 1540.1565–1567. This last canon anathematizes the doctrine of "double predestination."

grace, but that it is possible to oppose its irresistible nature through free will. On the one hand, we must affirm the precedence and infallibility of grace, for otherwise God would be subordinated to the creature. On the other hand, by emphasizing too heavily the precedence of grace, we risk annulling the role of the human will. This intriguing argument nuances the interrelation between grace and free will, which are not mutually exclusive but rather mutually inclusive. To favor nature against grace, we would incur the error of Pelagius and, conversely, we would incur the error of Luther by favoring grace against nature and free will. Rather, as Cardinal Journet states, "It is not only God *and* man, grace *and* freedom, but God *through* man, grace *through* freedom, that does the good act."[44]

However, the question bears repeating: how do grace and free will work together, or better yet, how is free will rightly subordinated to grace? Two theological schools debated on this matter in such a vehement manner that the pope himself had to intervene in order to put an end to the interminable dispute. On the one side was the Dominican school, represented by the Spanish theologian Domingo Báñez, who followed the teachings of St. Augustine and St. Thomas Aquinas. On the other side was the Jesuit school, represented by Portuguese theologian Luis de Molina, who had studied Aquinas but was not shy in departing from his thought.

Báñez described the efficacy of grace in terms of "physical predetermination," which obliged man's will. Molina

---

[44] Journet, *Meaning of Grace*, 33.

defended the truth of human freedom in relation to the work of grace, and the link between the two was seen as a kind of "moral predetermination" of man's will by grace. The two schools confronted each other in such a way as to accuse one another of falling into heresy: Báñez was accused of falling into the error of Lutheranism and Calvinism, while Molina, of falling into the error of Pelagianism or at least semi-Pelagianism. In 1607, Pope Paul V ended this dispute, exonerating both sides of heresy and commanding that they cease to make that accusation of one another.[45] But what was truly at stake in this dispute?[46]

a) According to Báñez, grace determines the human will in such a way that God knows exactly what an individual man will or will not do. With a pure and infinite act of knowledge, God knows everything that has happened or will happen, and for this reason, everything is infallibly decreed by God. The will of man is *physically* determined by grace, in the sense that grace affects and guides man's freedom *from within* himself. This teaching is called "*predetermining divine decrees*," in which "God determines from eternity that this man, under this particular circumstance, would act in such a way that he would receive instantly the 'irresistible grace' that determines him to act."[47]

---

[45] Cf. DH 1997.

[46] Cf. O'Callaghan, *God Ahead of Us*, 20–21.

[47] Juan Cruz Cruz, "Predestination as Transcendent Teleology: Molina and the First Molinism," in *A Companion to Luis de Molina*, ed. Matthias Kaufmann and Alexander Aichele (Leiden: Brill, 2013), 98.

b) According to Molina, grace does not determine the will of man, but works in such a way that man's freedom is respected, and predestination is decreed on the basis of human merits, foreseen by God from all eternity. An important distinction was introduced in this dispute, between *ante praevisa merita* (before the foreseen merits) and *post praevisa merita* (after the foreseen merits) of man. According to Molina, God infallibly decrees His predestination *post praevisa merita*, so that human freedom is fully respected, and man is coauthor of his salvation. God can do so because in His knowledge there is also a kind of middle knowledge—the *scientia media*—that allows Him to foresee man's response, knowing already all future happenings, and thus to act accordingly. In Molina's view, God's grace favors man's response, exercising a moral influence on his will.

Both theories were insufficient to express wholly the mystery of cooperation of grace and freedom. Báñez seems to overlook man's freedom, and he is often accused of falling into predestinationism. Molina, in order to defend the cooperation of free will, paves the way for a return of semi-Pelagianism: the movement from sufficient grace to efficacious grace would be made by man's decision to cooperate with God. Molina, in fact, had rejected the *praemotio physica*—a physical pre-motion of the will by grace. The point is that grace has of course an indisputable priority: God's initiative always comes first, and this supernatural gift is always efficacious, independent of man's disposition and choice. Freedom is respected and is never bent down by God's decision.

One aspect of this mystery was hardly mentioned, which would have greatly enlightened the discourse: love, which is the reason God grants us grace. Grace is always efficacious—even if given in such a way as to incur its possible rejection from man (that is, acting *sufficiently*)—and it always respects man's freedom, because God does all with love. Love is a strength of attraction to grace: it makes man capable and well-disposed to freely accept grace and adhere to it. The one struggling by his free will is gently conquered by love. St. Augustine had already seen this suavity of love that moves man toward the direction of grace while respecting his free will. The centrality of his argument in *Grace and Free Will* was exactly this: a "free gentleness of love"—"*liberalis suavitas amoris*"[48]—by which God "seduces" man and invites him, even irresistibly, to salvation. In this way, St. Augustine preserves the dignity of human freedom as well as the priority and excellence of grace, which leads infallibly to salvation.

3. Grace and Free Will: A Mystery of Mutual Cooperation

Another effective means of resolving this intriguing dispute *de auxiliis* is to turn our attention to the words of the prophet Jeremiah in the book of Lamentations (5:21): "Make us come back to you, O Lord, and we will come back." The divine actions that lead us along the way back to God are efficacious and preeminent, yet do not suspend the action of

---

[48] See Agostino Trapè, *Introduzione alla dottrina della grazia* in *Grazia e libertà*, vol. 2 (Roma: Città Nuova Editrice, 1990), 138–47.

free will. This passage from the Holy Scriptures is so significant that the Council of Trent referred to it in a canon about the doctrine of justification, quoting the prophet Zechariah as well: "When it is said in Sacred Scripture: 'Return to me and I will return to you' (Zech 1:3), we are reminded of our freedom; but when we reply: 'Restore us to yourself, O Lord, that we may be restored' (Lam 5:21), we acknowledge that God's grace precedes us."[49]

We may additionally expand our thoughts on the inscrutable relation between grace and free will by taking into account the wise considerations of Cardinal Journet.[50] He explains this relation as a circle, inside of which we have to place God and man, grace and free will. Moreover, a great light is shed on this circle, if we consider—in the view of the Swiss cardinal—the structure of the good act and of the evil act. In the good act, God is always the principal cause and man the secondary one. God's initiative enables our good actions. On the contrary, in the evil act, God is never the cause of it: He is only the natural cause of man's being but never the One who causes an evil action.

Homo prima causa mali—man is the first cause of evil. That is, evil comes from man's will, and thus he is the first (and last) cause of moral evil: the only thing he can do altogether "on his own" is *no-thing*. Unfortunately, on his own, man can destroy or annihilate the divine visitation of grace. Therefore, the cooperation of sufficient and

---

[49] DH 1525.
[50] Journet, *Meaning of Grace*, 37–43.

efficacious grace with man's freedom is seen by Journet in the words of the prophet Hosea (13:9): "Your destruction comes from you, O Israel: from me alone comes your help." These words of the prophet are well applicable to each soul, if we understand Israel in a figurative manner.

Sufficient grace is given to all, so that every person may be directed to God. Nonetheless, there are also exceptional cases in which a man is suddenly overwhelmed by an efficacious grace, an irresistible movement, as happened with St. Paul on the way to Damascus. God can therefore privilege some people with an efficacious grace, as he did particularly with our Lady, in order to preserve her from original sin and to enable her to become the mother of the Incarnate Word. In this regard, Journet comments: "The normal process is a series of graces that can be resisted but that if accepted will lead to one that is irresistible, victorious—a grace that will make me produce the good act, and I will thank God for giving me the strength to do so."[51]

This thought of Cardinal Journet elucidates well enough another issue about grace and free will, which arose with the Jansenists—followers of Bishop Cornelius Jansen (1585–1683).[52] Reacting against Molina, the Jansenists argued that there is no sufficient grace, claiming St. Augustine in support of their position. According to their theory, grace would be efficacious only, and would not be given to

---

[51] Journet, *Meaning of Grace*, 39.

[52] On Jansenism, see Nigel Abercrombie, *The Origins of Jansenism* (Oxford: Clarendon Press, 1936).

all men. Pagans, Jews, heretics, and others of this sort do not receive any assistance from Jesus Christ, but have only a bare and weak will, from which one may infer that they have no sufficient grace.[53] The denial of sufficient grace was strongly voiced by Jansenists who wished to avoid the danger of incurring any taint of Pelagianism. "Sufficient grace" was understood by Jansenists as an initial grace that suffices, *per se*, for actions, and this to them was detestable, since it would pave the way for introducing the discretion of man's will—to the extent of making even efficacious grace inefficacious. They composed the following famous prayer: "From sufficient grace deliver us, O Lord," as this kind of grace "is not so much useful as pernicious."[54]

Lastly, this mutual and mysterious relation between grace and free will, in this interesting dispute, becomes even clearer if we step back to see the big picture, that is, if we consider freedom as the power to choose good and to be inclined always to it. We have already made a distinction between free will as the *faculty of choosing* and freedom as a *state of liberty*.[55] Following up on this, it is also important to recall the concept of *delivered freedom*, i.e., of human freedom that has radically been liberated from sin and enriched by the gift of divine grace. It is because of this supernatural

---

[53] Cf. DH 2305.

[54] DH 2306. The Jansenists denied sufficient grace because they believed it put man in the position of effectuating his own salvation. In fact, their position implies a denial of free will and man's capacity to cooperate with God.

[55] Cf. O'Callaghan, *God Ahead of Us*, 126.

deliverance in Christ's Blood that man can freely be directed towards God. It is divine grace that empowers man's freedom and restores its lost dignity. By grace, free will is brought back to its status of freedom: a human capacity to choose God freely, the supreme and beatifying good.

This discourse may sound quite distant from our current understanding of man's freedom. But to reject the moral good, and ultimately God, and to choose idols is not an advance towards true liberation; it neither makes man great, nor makes him greater than he actually is. It is God who gives sense to our freedom, because it is only when we choose the good that we are free. Evil enslaves our will, but when the will is enabled by grace to adhere to the good, man can be truly free, without being subjugated by sin or slavery of any sort. From grace, we start to understand the true meaning of human freedom, one that is delivered from bondage.

The Mystery of Non-Election or Reprobation

Besides the mystery of predestination—the mystery of eternal election in God of those who will be saved—another doctrine is to be discussed: the mystery of non-election of those who will be eternally lost. This doctrine of "non-destination" was early defined by theologians as "reprobation."[56] The Synod of Quierzy in 853—already quoted above—established the consequence for those who rejected God's call to salvation: they are subjected to God's eternal decree of

---

[56] Cf. Schmaus, *Dogma*, 6–8.

reprobation. The Synod declares that if men do not drink the cup of salvation, which is the Blood of our Lord, they are not healed.[57] The Synod continues:

> The others, whom by the judgment of justice he left in the "mass of perdition," however, he knew would perish; but he did not predestine that they would perish; because he is just, however, he predestined eternal punishment for them. And on account of these we speak of only one predestination of God, which pertains either to the gift of life or to the retribution of justice.[58]

The wicked, who warrant their eternal punishment, as clearly taught by Jesus in the Gospel (see among others Mt 25:41), perish only because they were not able to be good:[59] this is a magisterial teaching on eternal reprobation by the Synod of Valencia in 855. Effectively, there is a substantial difference between those who were predestined to salvation and those who, out of their malice, remain part of the *massa damnata*. This difference is laid out by the Synod of Valencia: "In the election of those who are to be saved, the mercy of God precedes the merited good. In the condemnation of those who are to be lost, the evil they have deserved precedes the just judgement of God."[60]

---

[57] Cf. DH 624.
[58] DH 621.
[59] Cf. DH 627.
[60] DH 628.

The Council of Trent presupposes all these doctrinal statements and adds something particular in regards to Calvin's teaching on predestination. It condemned the view that the wicked, who are not predestined to salvation by grace, are consequently "predestined to evil by God's power."[61] Yet the doctrine of the reprobation of people who do not cooperate with God's grace is to be held as a truth revealed by God—*de fide*—reiterated constantly by the ordinary and universal Magisterium of the Church.[62]

At the end of this pathway through a very challenging topic, we come to this conclusion: despite our own natural inclination to resist the idea of damnation, we must admit that some people will not be saved, while some others will, not because of an arbitrary judgement of God, but solely due to the mystery of iniquity subverting man's freedom. An eternal plan of predestination in Christ of all things and of all men has been laid out by God and revealed in Christ. All peoples, by the indispensable aid of divine grace, are invited to accept the eternal call to salvation, which is a call to be in the likeness of Christ, and in Him to become children of God. Since freedom is real and not only apparent, man can even choose eternal damnation. Hence, we believe in the predestination of some to grace and glory and in the reprobation of others, due, again, to their lack of merits and to the rejection of divine grace. While grace is a gift that precedes man's disposition and

---

[61] DH 1567.

[62] Sceffczyk, *Katholische Dogmatik*, 226.

response, condemnation is a chastisement that follows man's evil works.

This finally enables us to consider, once more, that man's will without grace is completely vulnerable and defectible. In a world such as ours, where evil seems to predominate, and man continues to push the boundaries of it further and further, attempting to emancipate himself from God, no solution would be offered to its disastrous decay. However, it is not unjust or illogical that God would create a world in which evil is permissible and man receives retribution on account of his own works: it merely shows the transience of this creation and the fact that we are pilgrims in this world. In any case, such a precariousness witnesses to the need of divine grace.

3

Justification as the Happening and Realization of Divine Grace

WE NOW FOCUS OUR ATTENTION on the beginning of grace —on that divine process by which grace is granted to man. This grace-giving process is called "justification," as St. Paul refers to it in the Letter to the Romans (8:30). Continuing our discourse from the previous chapter, where we discussed the mystery of eternal predestination, we come now to understand the *call* of God, that is, the gift of conformity to Christ, for those who, chosen ahead of time, become true images of his Son, so that Christ might be the First Born among many brethren (see Rom 8:29).

St. Paul says: "He called those he intended for this; those he called he justified" (Rom 8:30). The original word used here is *edikaíosen*—to render just or innocent, free and righteous. Justification is the work of grace that renders man capable of passing from the death of sin to life in the First Born, Christ, so as to become adopted children of God made anew by grace—a new creation. Hence, justification is similar to sanctification. The whole process of rendering man just aims at transforming thoroughly a human person into a child of light, to free him from the slavery of sin, to make him an inheritor of eternal life, to fashion him holy and spotless before God in charity (see Eph 1:4–5).

Justification as a Divine Process

In the title of this new chapter, we stated that justification is the "happening" of divine grace. The verb "to happen"—whose root is the noun "hap"—suggests the idea of something that takes place in time, a temporal event. Justification is indeed an event that occurs at a specific moment in time; in a way, it recapitulates time and inaugurates its fullness for a person regenerated by God's grace. However, we must be careful: grace is not merely an event, it is a re-creation of man according to God's plan of salvation. Because of that, grace is a participation in an uncreated gift, God Himself, in time. The happening of grace coincides with the realization of grace. The "happening" points to the historical moment of grace, while "realization" points to the process of the giving of grace.

We can define justification as a divine action by which God delivers a creature from the state of sin and leads it to the state of grace (Rom 8:30). This perspective highlights the active aspect of this supernatural process. On the part of the creature, justification is the action by which divine and sanctifying justice is received, "being justified freely by his grace" (Rom 3:24), underscoring the passive aspect of justification. Moreover, we can also distinguish between justification as an infusion of grace in those who do not possess it because of a simple privation that has no note of guilt (as in our first parents, Adam and Eve, the Angels, and the Blessed Virgin Mary) and justification as an infusion of grace in those who do not possess it because of a positive privation (as in the justification of a sinner, who is washed, sanctified, and justified in the name of the Lord and of the Holy Spirit: see 1 Cor 6:11). Besides this, there is also the justification which increases the infused justice already present within a soul, according to the words of St. John: "he that is just, let him be justified still: and he that is holy, let him be sanctified still" (Rev 22:11).

Hence, justification is truly a passage from the state of sin to a new condition, the state of grace, which is the sanctification of the soul, of the whole human life. From this reality, we can define the original grace given as *sanctifying* grace. It is important to understand this interior transformation wrought by grace. St. Thomas helps us to understand it by distinguishing a point of departure—*whence*—and a point of arrival—*whereto*—in this process (in Latin, *terminus a quo* and *terminus ad quem*). Thus, St. Thomas says:

> And because movement is named after its term "whereto" rather than from its term "whence," the transmutation whereby anyone is changed by the remission of sins from the state of ungodliness to the state of justice, borrows its name from its term "whereto," and is called "justification of the ungodly."[63]

---

[63] St. Thomas Aquinas, *Summa Theologiae* (hereafter, *ST*) I-II, Q. 113, art. 1.

The movement towards justification has two features: a) a *true remission* of sins, which not only covers up, but cancels sin; b) an *inner renewal and sanctification* of the soul, whereby man is indeed a "new creation," i.e., "from unjust man becomes just, and from an enemy a friend, that he may be 'an heir in hope of eternal life' (Titus 3:7)."[64] Therefore, justification is not extrinsic, but intrinsic, excluding not only the error of the Protestants—as we will shortly study— but also any kind of middle way, as for instance espoused by Martin Bucer (1491–1551), a former Dominican who embraced the Protestant Reformation. Bucer supported the doctrine of a double justification, one exterior by the imputation of Christ and the other interior by the adhering gift of grace.

More radical than a middle way was the doctrine of Michael Baius (1513–1589). Baius affirmed incorrectly that justification consisted formally only in obedience to the commandments of God, without any remission of sins and the infusion of sanctifying grace. This thesis was condemned by the Council of Trent.[65]

Faith is central in the initial stage of justification. In fact, "man is justified by faith, without the works of the law" (Rom 3:28). It is theological faith which disposes the heart to welcome sanctifying grace, entirely gratuitous and unmerited, producing the supernatural effects of justification. According to St. Augustine, grace precedes faith as

---

[64] Council of Trent, *Decree on Justification*: DH 1528.
[65] DH 1942.

it precedes the will as well.[66] St. Thomas Aquinas adds
that it is grace which *produces* faith—*gratia facit fidem*, "not
only when faith begins anew to dwell in man, but also as
long as faith lasts."[67] Hence, the very first grace is faith, and
faith is the disposition to be justified. The primacy is God's,
and, absolutely speaking, this also holds true of the primacy
of grace in regard to man. The Council of Trent, in the
decree on justification, will define this faith as "prevenient
grace," which disposes a sinner to assent and to cooperate
with the grace of justification.[68]

Martin Luther's View on Justification

The leading idea of Luther on the nature of justification
derives from his concept of original sin. For Luther, the
sin of Adam and Eve had so corrupted human nature that
nothing was left intact, retaining nothing of its human aspect. Original sin had perverted the intelligence and the
will of man, affecting the sensible sphere as well. Original
sin devastated man's nature to such an extent that neither
baptism nor any other divine aid could eradicate its effects.
Thus, humans are prisoners of this sin and of its effects,
especially concupiscence—a disordered desire to seek after
sensible goods. This last thought, according to Luther's understanding, was the "driving force," overwhelming man's
life, representing something of an unbreakable chain in his

---

[66] Cf. *De dono perseverantiae*, 16, 41.

[67] *ST* II-II, Q. 4, art. 4, ad 3.

[68] DH 1525.

life. Luther's principal error was his inability to distinguish properly original sin from the effects of concupiscence. Because of the preponderance of concupiscence and its life-long duration till the point of death, the German Reformer was keen on the idea of the perpetuity of original sin upon man's soul, being resistant even to the grace of justification.[69]

During his theological formation, Luther was educated in a nominalistic[70] environment. For this reason, he easily began to reject the concept of grace as *habitus*—a habit producing an ontological as well as inner sanctification of the soul. Luther attributed the invention of a *habitus* to the "rancid philosopher"[71] Aristotle, but ultimately, he was

---

[69] The same identification of original sin with the perpetual infection of concupiscence, to the point of judging that "concupiscence and lust hath of itself the nature of sin," is made in Article 9 of the Anglican Community. In general, the Thirty-Nine Articles are modelled on the Lutheran vision and repudiate teachings and practices that Protestants condemned in the Catholic Church. They date back to the year 1563, drawn up under Elizabeth I and based on the work of Thomas Cranmer.

[70] Nominalism is a philosophy according to which concepts or words do not express the reality as such, but are only sounds and bare intellectual representations of reality, used for convenience to communicate, but deprived of their interior essence, which identifies the entities that exist. For Nominalism, there is a void between reality and intelligence. Reality would be beyond intellectual knowledge. This nominalist stream easily flows into the river of Empiricism and finally of Pragmatism.

[71] This was said in making his observations on Peter Lombard's *Sentences*, dist. 17: Martin Luther, *Werke* (abbreviated WA for *Weimar Ausgabe*), vol. 9 (Weimar, 1983), 43, 45.

rejecting the classical teaching of the Scholastics, particularly that of St. Thomas. However, the word itself was not rejected as such. In fact, *habitus*, in his new vision, is actually original sin, which cannot be destroyed but remains as it is. Man is only *declared* just by being "covered" with the justice of Christ, but inwardly he remains a sinner. His sins are not imputed to him, in the sense that they are held as cancelled, while in fact they are still present but concealed by the mantle of grace. In Luther's mind, this makes the role played by faith comprehensible.

Thus, Luther believed that man was not free to avoid sin. Original sin permanently enslaves the human will. However, this does not mean that a man no longer formally has the power of choice. Luther simply is not interested in the metaphysical question of man's power to choose (*liberum arbitrium*—free will, as defined by St. Augustine). What truly matters to him is to know how the question of the salvific action of God might be answered.[72] It is basically an existential theological orientation that, *de facto*, brought Luther to support the denial of the possibility of not choosing evil and sin. Luther draws the following conclusion: humans are in a depraved condition, not capable of choosing anything but sin. Since freedom of choice is permanently bent, the best men can hope for is to be not judged as sinners due to the free gift of God.

That being said, we come to understand the fundamental role of faith in Luther's assumption. Faith, for Luther,

---

[72] Cf. Schmaus, *Dogma*, 17.

is a cordial trust in God whereby Christ is made present.[73] Precisely, "faith is a confidence of heart (*fiducia cordis*) through Christ in God," so that "1. Faith is a divine gift, by which I believe (*qua credo*) in Christ. 2. God considers (*reputat*) this imperfect faith as perfect justice."[74] To this it is to be added that "*fides imputatur ad iustitiam propter Christum*"—"faith is imputed as justice because of Christ."[75]

---

[73] Martin Luther, *In epistolam S. Pauli ad Galatas Commentarius (3:6)* in WA 40:366.

[74] Luther, *In epistolam S. Pauli ad Galatas Commentarius*, 366, 5. Luther expands on this point: "For this faith in Christ, God does not see the sin that hitherto remains in me. As long as I live in this body, indeed sin is in me. In the meantime, Christ protects me under the shadow of his wings and brings over me the extensive heaven, that is remission of sins, under which I can safely walk. . . . In truth, God dissimulates these sins that he sees, as if they were not sins (*quasi non essent peccata*). And this is made by that imputation by faith whereby I begin to apprehend Christ, by whom God considers the imperfect justice as perfect justice and sin as non-sin, although it is a true sin." Luther, *In epistolam S. Pauli ad Galatas Commentarius*, 367, 15. Let us bear in mind that Luther is commenting on the Letter of St. Paul to the Galatians 3:6, where the Apostle speaks of Abraham's example and says: "He put his faith in God, and it was reputed to him unto justice." The Greek verb to express the English "to repute" or "to consider" is *elogíste* from *logízomai*, in the sense of counting, or keeping a mental record. God kept in mind the justice of Abraham and saved him because of his faith. But Abraham was truly justified, or sanctified, and not, as Luther insinuates, only accounted as just by the mere hiding of his sins. Justice was truly given to Abraham, otherwise he would not have been blessed. Luther's interpretation is far beyond the text.

[75] Ibid., 366, 25.

By this *fiducial* faith, Christ becomes united with the believer and consequently a "joyful bargain" ("*admirabile commercium*") is made: Christ takes on my sin and gives me His justice.[76] This faith enables man to receive the justice *of* Christ. Luther understands this genitive *of Christ* in an objective manner: the justice received by a sinner is formally the same justice by which Christ is holy and just. For this reason, Luther will speak of *iustitia Christi aliena*—which is a justice that cannot belong to man, but rather, to Christ. This justice is only exterior and does not adhere to one's soul. It is only a "forensic justice"—given as an amnesty in a court after a juridical process, because it does not reach man's heart.

Justice is exterior in regard to man's life, but efficacious with reference to his eternal salvation. It is a matter of joining two issues here: for Luther, on one side, man is not interiorly holy, but, on the other side, he is justified. Without noticing the contradiction, Luther argued that a man is at the same time just and a sinner. Man is "one and the same time a sinner and a righteous person (*simul iustus et peccator*). He is a sinner in fact, but a righteous person by the sure reckoning and promise of God that he will continue to deliver him from sin until he has completely

---

[76] This idea was developed by Luther principally in his treatise *On the Freedom of the Christian*, WA 7. The young Luther's idea of "exchange" shifted, during his maturity, towards the theology of the Cross: here, there is the exchange between the majesty of God and the sinfulness of man.

cured him."[77] To make use of an analogy, man is a sick person who is going to be healed, but he never is, because he cannot be healed due to the irremediable devastation of sin. No medicine is fit to this purpose, although grace is present. Faith as a fiducial trust that one day healing will come about is the remedy.

One final point: Faith contains in itself all possible good works, either because the very good work is faith itself or because the good works are so united to one another, as to render it impossible to separate them from the act of faith, just as it is impossible to separate heat and light from fire. Therefore, Luther does not deny the necessity of charity and good works, but he conflates these with faith. Charity is like a mirror of that faith which firmly and fiducially believes in justification. Consequently, the Reformers do not deny the necessity of doing good and the necessity of a moral life; rather, their concern regards solely the incorporation of good works into the fiducial faith, into "faith alone." To incorporate charity into faith, Luther particularly had to deny the existence either of an *implicit* faith—that essential requirement of believing in God's existence and in his retribution (see Heb 11:6) or of faith as uninformed by charity—faith possessed by a man, after his justification, who is in a state of mortal sin.

For the German Reformer, faith is described by a special concept, always pointing to it as trust in the salvation of Christ, and this to such an extent as to exclude the *fides quae creditur*—the faith as a plurality of doctrines to believe.

---

[77]   WA 56:272, 3–21.

Luther postulated the existence and the necessity only of the *fides qua*—the faith by which I believe in God.[78] Hence, faith is only and always the human act of faith, independently from its content. An exaggeration of this view leads undoubtedly to the absence even of the reasoning behind believing in God.

Schematically, we can summarize Luther's assumptions in the following points:

1. Luther understands justification essentially as an extrinsic condonation of all guilt, which does not enable any remission of sins; the process of justification does not cause any infusion of habitual (from habit—*habitus*) or sanctifying grace, nor of any supernatural virtues: it is only by God's favor that the justice of Christ is put on man.

2. For the remission/hiding of sin, no other interior disposition is required than faith as a trust that one's sins will be forgiven.

3. The justice received by Christ is the same for everyone and does not grow up on account of good works, nor may it be lost on account of bad ones, as Calvinists would add, except for the sin of unbelief. Justice is always exterior and never possessed by man as his own. Good works are not necessary for salvation, not because they do not matter but because they are one with faith and exist only within faith.

---

[78] Cf. Scheffczyk, *Katholische Dogmatik*, 486–91.

4. Humans can never know by faith whether they are effectively justified, but having a fiducial faith is the only way to hold strongly to its certitude, believing that man is justified indeed.

The Answer of the Council of Trent

During the Sixth Session, in January 1547, the Council of Trent issued a Decree on Justification, to confirm all points of Catholic faith put into question by Luther and his fellow disciples, condemning all heretical statements. First, as already mentioned above, the Council laid down the necessity of justification, its preparation, its nature, and its causes. Among the causes of justification, the Council distinguished: a) the *final cause*, which is the glory of God and of Christ and life everlasting; b) the *efficient cause*: the merciful God who gratuitously cleanses and sanctifies; c) the *meritorious cause*: the only begotten Son of God, who merited this grace by his Passion and death on the Cross, making satisfaction to God the Father on our behalf; d) the *instrumental cause*: the sacrament of baptism, that "sacrament of faith," without which no one can be justified, and finally e) the *formal cause*: the justice of God, precisely the direct opposite of Luther's belief—"not that by which he (God) is himself just, but that by which he makes us just."[79] Justification can never be *iustitia Christi aliena*.

---

[79] This doctrine is part of the chapter 7 of the Decree (DH 1529) and is formulated also as canon 10 (DH 1560).

Justification as the Happening and Realization of Grace

1. Justification Is Gratuitous through Faith

The Decree of Trent then elucidates the correct understanding of the sinner's gratuitous justification through faith. Firstly, to say that we are justified through faith means that "faith is the beginning of man's salvation"[80] and that without faith it is impossible to please God (see Heb 11:6); secondly, to say that we are justified gratuitously—*only through faith*, i.e., without any human cooperation, and not through *faith alone*—means that nothing preceding justification, neither faith nor works, can merit the grace of justification; if something else than grace preceded justification, in the sense of meriting it, grace would no longer be grace (Rom 11:6).[81]

However, the gratuitousness of man's justification through faith does not imply that one should consider himself exempt from the observance of the commandments, or conversely—something very pertinent today—that the observance of God's commandments is impossible for the justified.[82] "For God does not command the impossible, but when he commands he 'admonishes you to do what you can and to pray for what you cannot do,' and he helps you to accomplish it."[83] From this, the Council draws the consequence that "nobody should flatter himself with faith alone (can. 9, 19, 20), thinking that by faith alone he is made an heir and will obtain the inheritance even if he does not

---

[80] *Rituale Romanum*, Order of Baptism, n. 1: DH 1532.

[81] Cf. DH 1532.

[82] Cf. DH 1536.

[83] Ibid. Here St. Augustine, *De natura et gratia*, 43, is quoted.

'suffer with Christ in order that he may also be glorified with him' (cf. Rom 8:17)."[84]

2. Faith Not Informed and the Doctrine of Merit

Moreover, contrary to Luther's assumption, the Council states that each mortal sin causes the loss of grace but not of faith. The grace of justification, once received, is lost not only through unbelief (cf. also can. 27), which causes the loss of faith itself, but also by any other mortal sin, even if, in this case, faith is not lost.[85] By the faith still remaining, although not formed by grace and charity, man can draw near to God, making a good confession, and so receive sanctifying grace once more.

Lastly, the Council makes the point on merit in relation to good works. One must perform good works to obtain eternal life, and they are not identical with faith. St. James clearly speaks of works as distinguished from theological faith; it is because of good works that one can prove his faith (see Jam 2:18). The first of these works is charity, which is the mother of all good works. In fact, "faith works through charity" (Gal 5:6), "for faith without hope and charity neither unites a man perfectly with Christ nor makes him a living member of his body."[86]

Therefore, faith requires man's cooperation—an idea truly hostile to the German Reformer. For Luther, as we

---

[84]   Ibid.

[85]   Cf. DH 1544.

[86]   DH 1531.

have said, man is incapable of any good since his nature is wounded, not to mention his inability to cooperate with grace in his own salvation after the first justification. Contrary to this position, the Council of Trent reiterates that Christ continuously infuses strength into the justified, and this strength "precedes, accompanies, and follows their good works, which, without it, could in no way be pleasing to God and meritorious (can 2)."[87]

Good works are crowned by supernatural merits, which are nothing more than an increase of sanctifying grace as well as that of eternal life and glory.[88] Merits are not the fruit of man's ability, but rather a grace for cooperating with God, and above all a reward from the Lord for the good accomplished under the assistance of grace. In fact, St. Augustine says that "God, when he rewards our actions, crowns his own gifts."[89] A merit is then a supplement of grace. Writes O'Callaghan: "Every meritorious act brings about an increase in sanctifying grace and the infused virtues; the believer becomes ever more *alter Christus, ipse Christus*, 'another Christ, Christ himself.'"[90] We can sum this up with a statement by Cardinal Journet: "Our merits are from God and Christ as first cause, and from us as second cause—God gives us, in Christ, the power to assent."[91]

---

[87] DH 1546; cf. can. 32, DH 1582.

[88] Cf. DH 1582.

[89] *Epistola* 194, 5, 19.

[90] O'Callaghan, *God Ahead of Us*, 109.

[91] Journet, *Meaning of Grace*, 70.

Luther could not bear the idea that sinful man could merit something. Because his vision of human nature was thoroughly pessimistic, he excluded the possibility of any good on man's part, except that which comes from a firm, fiducial faith in Christ's salvific work— "a confidence in the divine mercy that remits sins on account of Christ."[92] Rightly was this anathematized by Trent. For Luther, a man can even sin if he performs good works with a view to eternal reward.[93] The Council rejects this decisively:

> If anyone says that for the good works performed in God (cf. Jn 3:21) the just ought not to expect and hope for an eternal reward from God through his mercy and the merits of Jesus Christ, if they persevere to the end in doing good and in keeping the divine commandments (cf. Mt 10:22; 24:13), let him be anathema.[94]

In conclusion, the Council says that "no one can be justified unless he faithfully and firmly accepts this Catholic doctrine on justification."[95]

Sanctifying Grace as a Created, Interior, and Permanent Entity

We now have a clearer idea about divine grace, having explained the process of justification. Grace is a gift given by

---

[92] DH 1562.

[93] DH 1581.

[94] DH 1576. See also can. 32: DH 1582 and DH 1538.

[95] DH 1550.

God and conferred on man by the sacrament of baptism, through which the process of grace is realized. As a gift given, grace is not God Himself (in this case we would fall into the error of pantheism) but a reality substantially distinct from Him, that is, a created reality, whereas God is an uncreated Being. The Scholastics thus make a basic distinction between these two realities: sanctifying grace is *gratia creata* (created grace), while God, specifically the Holy Spirit the Sanctifier, the giver of grace, is *gratia increata* (uncreated grace).

It is interesting to know that for St. Augustine the Holy Spirit is *donum Dei*, the gift of God. More precisely, he says that the Holy Spirit is "a gift eternally, but a thing that has been given in time."[96] Grace is a gift of the One who is the Gift of God. Another Father of the Church, St. Cyril of Alexandria, explains this relation between the Holy Spirit and grace as a created power: the Holy Spirit is the one who forms Christ in us, and with sanctification and justice He puts on us a divine form.[97]

This distinction within grace helps us to see, on one hand, the supernatural essence of sanctifying grace and its intimate unity with God, a unity bringing us into a divine relationship with God, and, on the other hand, the existence of a substantial distinction from God, in which grace adheres to the soul of a baptized person, raising him

---

[96] *De Trinitate*, 5, 16, 17: "Nam sempiterne Spiritus donum, temporaliter autem donatum."

[97] *In Isaiam*, 1:4.

up into a supernatural state, the state of divine sonship, rendering him an heir of the kingdom of heaven. Grace brings, as we have mentioned, the gift of faith, hope, and charity, and all the infused supernatural virtues.[98]

Hence, when we call grace "created," we are indicating that, so far from being something uncertain, vague, or abstract, it pertains to God Himself; it is divine insofar as it is divinely communicated within the soul by God Himself. Cardinal Journet helps us come to a better understanding of this created entity: "In me there is a ray of his (God's) life and his love, that is to say, a finite *participation* in the divine nature; but grace in me is directed immediately on to the *infinite depths of God*. You see the mystery, simultaneously finite and infinite in character."[99] Uncreated grace and created grace work together simultaneously in producing the supernatural effects in souls. With an enlightening analogy, Journet explains this simultaneity: the uncreated Spirit is given in created grace, as the sun is given in its rays.[100]

From this, two additional qualities of divine and sanctifying grace are brought forth.

1. Grace is *interior*—that is, an inward gift that renews one's life. Grace likewise produces a transformation from the death of sin to life, a life growing ever more abundantly as it grows

---

[98] Cf. DH 1530.

[99] Journet, *Meaning of Grace*, 24.

[100] Journet, *Meaning of Grace*, 26.

in grace. This is far from Luther's teaching of a mere *iustitia Christi aliena*. Such a justice belongs not to the sinner but solely to Christ, and for this reason it is given only exteriorly, in the same manner as a mantle warms up a person, hiding his nakedness—that is, his sins. A person in grace is instead a temple of God, wherein the Holy Spirit dwells (see 1 Cor 3:16).

2. Grace is *permanent*. It is a habit (*habitus*), which "re-dresses" man's soul and by which he is adopted as a child of God. For this reason, sanctifying grace is also termed *habitual* grace. Justification is a new generation, a new birth, "by means of the cleansing water of rebirth and by renewing us with the Holy Spirit which (God) poured over us through Jesus Christ our Savior" (Titus 3:5–6). Grace, therefore, is not a transient quality of the soul but a new status of our soul, regenerating us supernaturally. Grace adheres to our soul permanently, as long as it is not rejected by committing mortal sin—a disobedience to God's law and love. Those who forfeit this grace after being justified are able to be "justified" again, through the sacrament of Penance and the merits of Christ.[101]

This permanence of habitual grace, then, is to be understood not as a moral permanence but as an ontological one: the

---

[101] DH 1542 and can. 29: DH 1579.

habitus of grace is not an aid[102] helping us to choose good and to avoid evil, but, once again, a reality which truly transforms our souls, raising them up to a new, supernatural condition.

Finally, sanctifying grace elevates the entire human being to a supernatural status, permeating his whole life and therefore all his faculties, such as intellect, will, and memory. This does not change the human properties of man's actions, both material and spiritual, but enables them to be fruitful for eternal life. Moreover, divine grace builds within man's life a "supernatural organism" made by the theological virtues of faith, hope, and charity, and the seven gifts of the Holy Spirit, as well as the fruits of the Holy Spirit and the Beatitudes. A new spiritual and supernatural existence is given to humans by divine grace. Faithfulness to it means having indeed the Holy Spirit working actively in us by these supernatural virtues and gifts of his love.[103]

Sanctifying Grace as Participation in the Divine Nature and Inhabitation of the Holy Trinity

Let us now focus on the effects of sanctifying grace, the communion with the divine nature and, consequently, the

---

[102] In the next chapter, we will study actual grace, which is an aid to our soul, but transient.

[103] We will not deal in this context specifically with the activity of theological virtues and gifts of the Holy Spirit in relation to divine grace. For this, I invite the reader to study the contribution of O'Callaghan, *God Ahead of Us*, 77–101. However, in the next chapter, we will examine the presence of the Holy Spirit in a soul in grace and the unique relation of grace with charity as well as with faith and hope.

dwelling of the Holy Trinity within the soul. Divine grace indeed institutes a living relationship with the Godhead. In the words of St. Bonaventure: "Grace is a gift by which the soul is perfected and transformed into the bride of Christ, the daughter of the eternal Father, and the temple of the Holy Spirit: all of which can be brought about only by the ennobling condescension and condescending nobility of the eternal Majesty through the gift of His grace."[104] St. Bonaventure's poetic words demonstrate how grace enables a dynamic relationship with God, one that animates the soul and draws her closer to the most Holy Trinity. I will describe this loving relationship in more detail in the following sections.

1. Partakers of the Divine Nature

One of the scriptural texts most expressive of the "new creation" realized by grace is that of St. Peter: we are made "partakers of the divine nature" (2 Pt 1:4). This mystery is truly incomprehensible to a human mind but nonetheless fascinating. Grace effects a *share* in God's own nature. The Greek word that St. Peter uses for "partakers" is *koinonoì* (from *koinonia*—communion), in the Latin translated as *consortes* (from *consors*, the same Latin word for "husband" and "wife"). Grace is communion (a common union) with the divine nature or better yet, a spousal relationship with God. In this relationship, God is the bridegroom and our soul the bride, united in a pact of immutable love, which is grace.

---

[104] St. Bonaventure, *Breviloquium*, part. V, c. 1, n. 2.

God's Abode with Man

Grace creates our friendship with God and enables us not only to become children of God (cf. Jn 1:12), but to be heirs, dwelling in His house. For this indwelling to occur, the Greek Fathers—as we have already seen—speak of a divinization of the soul by grace: a participation,[105] not effected by a moral imitation or a substantial transformation, but one of such intimacy in God's own life as to elevate man's soul to the heights of the Divinity, enabling him to see Him one day face to face (see 1 Cor 13:12).

St. Thomas Aquinas explains this ineffable mystery quite precisely. God, by His Holy Spirit, elevates the human soul to the supernatural state in order to admit it to live in communion with Him. Grace operates in man in a manner not superseding His nature, but rather respecting its very essence, rendering man a participant in God's divine nature. As St. Thomas says, "That which is substantially present in God becomes accidental in the soul of one who shares in divine goodness."[106] In another question of his *Summa*, Aquinas also says that grace, in some way, makes us truly like God: "Grace is caused in men from the presence of

---

[105] The notion of participation is a key to understanding the whole Christian mystery. We can define participation in the following manner: a relation between a partial ontological perfection and a total ontological perfection, i.e., absolute. In other words, participation outlines a metaphysical imitation, which is limited and caused by another, namely, a pure, unlimited, and non-caused perfection. The one who participates *in* is the partial perfection; the one who *is* participated is the pure and absolute perfection.
[106] *ST* I-II, Q. 110, art. 2.

God, in the same way as light in the air from the presence of the sun."[107]

2. The Inhabitation of the Triune God

The inhabitation of the Holy Trinity within the soul is the last magnificent mystery in our study of sanctifying grace. In this regard, we have the very words of our Lord Himself: "If anyone loves me he will keep my word, and my Father will love him, and we shall come to him and make our home with him" (Jn 14:23). Here the accent is on *love* rather than grace. This emphasis brings into focus the Franciscan lens, originating with Peter Lombard, which identifies grace with charity—contrary to St. Thomas's teaching—for both are produced by the same Author, the Holy Spirit. We shall tackle this intriguing question in the following chapter. For the moment, it is necessary to see the mystery of divine inhabitation as an extension of the one just discussed—our participation in the divine nature. Grace, in any case, enables us to share in the divine nature; conversely, God Himself, the Triune and infinite God, is present within the soul, but in a finite and created manner—by way of sanctifying grace.

The participation in the divine nature unites the soul to God in His deepest, innermost being. If we wish to make reference again to created and uncreated grace, we might say that, in the mystery of the inhabitation of the Holy Trinity, both work simultaneously. By the created gift of grace, one

---

[107] *ST* III, Q. 7, art. 13. See also O'Callaghan, *God Ahead of Us*, 67.

is able to be inhabited by God, but conversely, this same created gift does not effect this indwelling. Rather, the uncreated Gift of God Himself realizes this inhabitation. In other words, the Holy Spirit makes the Triune God dwell within the soul, whereas grace, that supernatural created quality, enables the soul to possess the presence of God dwelling within.[108]

Therefore, God the Holy Trinity is present within the soul. By participation through grace, the inner life of God is communicated to the soul. This means that in the soul the Father generates the Son and the Father and the Son breathe forth the Holy Spirit. By grace, the soul and its faculties of intellect and will become participants in these divine Trinitarian processions. The intellect, by grace, can draw ever closer to the infinite generation of the Son and know the Truth, the Logos, by abiding in Him; furthermore, the will is enflamed with the love by which the Holy Spirit is poured out, so that it can love with the same love by which God loves all things. This is a tremendous mystery which empowers our spiritual life. This inhabitation is intensified and vivified especially in the reception of Holy Communion. With the Son present within us under the sacramental species, the Father and the Holy Spirit are present as well: where the Son is, there likewise is present the Father and the Holy Spirit. Consequently, the life of the Holy Trinity within us grows to such an extent as to lead us easily into the mystical

---

[108] Cf. Journet, *Meaning of Grace*, 24–26.

dimension of Christian life. The ascetical and mystical aspects of Christian life are worked out by the same principle of sanctifying grace.

In fine, the indwelling of the Holy Trinity is the presence of God within the soul in the state of grace. This presence is a participation in God's divine nature. To speak in theological terms, it would be worth quoting extensively St. Thomas's description of the presence of the Holy Trinity within the soul:

> God is in all things by His essence, power, and presence, according to His one common mode, as the cause existing in the effects which participate in His goodness. Above and beyond this common mode, however, there is one special mode belonging to the rational nature wherein God is said to be present as the object known is in the knower, and the beloved in the lover. And since the rational creature by its operation of knowledge and love attains to God Himself, according to this special mode God is said not only to exist in the rational creature but also to dwell therein as in His own temple. So no other effect can be put down as the reason why the divine person is in the rational creature in a new mode, except sanctifying grace. Hence, the divine person is sent, and proceeds temporally only according to sanctifying grace.[109]

---

[109] *ST* I, Q. 43, art. 3.

God's Abode with Man

It is interesting to note the analogy made between God's presence within the soul and that of the beloved within the lover. This analogy makes reference to the aforementioned text of St. John: if one loves the Lord, the Holy Trinity will come and abide with him. Christian love is not sentimental but rather, it is the charity poured into our hearts by the Holy Spirit, as St. Paul proclaims (see Rom 5:5).

Only through Baptism, Children of God

It remains for us to speak about the consequences of justification before concluding our discourse on habitual grace. The process of justification has led us to see closely the work of divine grace: a *regeneration* of a man, born into original sin and reborn in grace, and a *sanctification* of the whole person, by which divine filiation with God the Father through Christ, the only Son, is accomplished in the Holy Spirit. This first and original justification is worked out by the sacrament of regeneration: holy baptism. Through it, the Christian dies to sin and is buried with Christ, in order to rise with Him to a new life (see Rom 6:1–4). Through baptism, the Holy Spirit enables the divine filiation of a child "reborn by the Spirit" (Jn 3:8). In fact, all those moved by the Holy Spirit are the sons of God, and this same Spirit that they receive renders them children of God, making them cry, "Abba, Father" (see Rom 8:14–15). The passage from Romans continues: "If we are children, we are heirs as well: heirs of God and coheirs with Christ, sharing in his suffering so as to share his glory" (8:17).

A creature, created in God's image and likeness, is even capable of becoming one of His sons. This divine filiation is the grace to be generated in Christ as a son, not through blood and flesh, but of God (see Jn 1:13). The Word was made flesh, such that those predestined in Him might be made children of God by the Holy Spirit. However, creatures become children of God and have a share in God's divine nature only through the sacrament of baptism, by the operation of the Holy Spirit. Outside this divine and supernatural filiation, there are no other means of becoming God's children.

The question then arises: Are baptized Christians the only ones who are children of God? Additionally, many say that all men and women, whatever be their faith, are children of God. Even non-religious people such as atheists, in a great embrace of mercy, are sometimes considered children of God. We can correctly answer the question if we answer a preliminary question: what does it mean to be a child of God?

First of all, we can think about being in a filial relationship with God in a broader sense. The book of Genesis teaches that man, prior to his fall, was created "in the image and likeness of God" (Gen 1:27). "For this reason," says O'Callaghan, "if anyone is a son or daughter of God in any way, this can only be on the basis of a sharing, through creation or redemption, in the Word's eternal and unique filiation."[110] There is only one Son, Christ. If anyone wants

---

[110] O'Callaghan, *God Ahead of Us*, 56.

to partake in God's life, one must, of necessity, draw near to this only Son. But to maintain that an unbaptized creature is a son of God is incorrect. Filiation, in its proper sense, requires generation: that is, the supernatural power of the Holy Spirit poured forth into man's soul to be a new creation in Christ. Filiation is realized only in the reception of sanctifying grace at baptism, because it gives the soul a *seal*, which allows the soul to become a child of God. Moreover, although baptism of desire is salvific,[111] it does not imprint onto the soul the character of the children of God.[112] The baptismal character carries out two effects: *conformity* with Christ and *distinction* from all others.[113]

This is one more reason to affirm the necessity of sacramental baptism,[114] according to the clear words of our Lord (see Jn 3:5, Mt 28:19–20, and Mk 16:15–16). We ought now to have that evangelical courage to proclaim the truth that only through baptism do we become children of God. This would surely animate the "new evangelization" of the Church, which otherwise might remain stagnant.

In conclusion, we might draw one last consequence from this discourse: grace is always and solely *Christian*. It is given by Christ; and only Christ, as true God and true man, is the mediator of this sanctifying gift. His sacred humanity is the efficacious instrument producing grace.

---

[111] That is, it yields the fruits of baptism even if it is not a sacrament. Cf. CCC 1258.

[112] Cf. St. Thomas, *In IV Sententiarum*, Dist. 4, Q. 1, art. 4.

[113] Ibid.

[114] Cf. CCC 1257.

As filiation can happen only through Him—because God has only one Son—grace can only have a Christian mark.

Nevertheless, God is willing to distribute His grace to every man, should he knock and ask (Mt 7:7). Non-Christians can also receive divine grace to be saved.[115] In the Dogmatic Constitution *Gaudium et Spes* (n. 22), the Second Vatican Council has indicated that Christ died for all men, which means that we should believe that God—in a manner known only to Him—offers to every man the possibility of encountering Christ in His Paschal Mystery. All men of all religions can surely be saved, but their salvation can occur only through Christ's grace and in relation to Christ's mystical body, the Church.[116] Through Him, with Him, and in Him: there is no grace other than Christ's grace of salvation.

---

[115] Cf. CCC 1260.

[116] On this issue the document of the Congregation for the Doctrine of Faith, *Dominus Iesus* (August 6, 2000), is truly enlightening.

4

Grace from the Perspective of the Receiver: Actual Grace and Its Implications

IN THIS PRESENT CHAPTER WE will tackle a new issue: we will consider divine grace insofar as it is received by man. Grace is one and—as already mentioned—a participation in God's intimate life. Yet we can consider grace in a twofold manner: grace in its essence, or grace in its operation upon the soul. Precisely for this reason, we can fundamentally distinguish between *grace as a created and inherent supernatural quality* of Christian life, which we have called sanctifying or habitual grace, and *grace as a divine help* to aid the soul in receiving and remaining in sanctifying grace—not only to be given momentarily, but to accompany the entirety of Christian life. This latter is called *actual grace*, referring to a divine motion, a salvific aid provided by God to assist us continuously.

Grace is not divided, but one. Thus, all the distinctions made will serve only to aid our attentive study of its effects upon us. In describing the theological implications of the effects of grace, the narrative of grace comes to be greatly enriched, for God never ceases to work marvels in bringing man from his state of disgrace and sin into a new state of grace and eternal life.

Actual Grace

In one of the questions of the *Summa Theologiae*, St. Thomas Aquinas asks whether man, by himself and without the aid of grace, can prepare himself for grace; in other words: is grace needed to receive that initial gift of grace, which we've seen as the process of justification?[117] If we attentively ponder the supernatural order and the way to dispose oneself for its reception, we must affirm with St. Thomas that grace *is* indeed necessary to prepare oneself for grace. Grace "moves" a person to be disposed to receive grace, continuing to accompany him so that he might always be open to its reception, lest it be lost through mortal sin. Furthermore, grace continually accompanies a person to its increase when a soul, living in the state of sanctifying grace, grows in virtue and merit.

We therefore give the name *actual grace* to the grace that moves the human will to consent to God's grace, not only preceding and following our good works, but even accompanying it after its completion. In this manner, actual grace prepares the human will as well as the whole person for the gift of habitual grace. In the words of the Angelic Doctor, we can reason accordingly: "In order that man prepare himself to receive this gift (habitual grace), it is not necessary to presuppose any further habitual gift in the

---

[117] *ST* I-II, Q. 109, art. 6.

soul, otherwise we should go on to infinity. But we must presuppose a gratuitous gift of God, Who moves the soul inwardly or inspires the good wish."[118]

This gratuitous gift is the grace of God that produces the inward movement of the human will towards the accomplishment of a good action. The inflow of grace ceases after the deed is completed. Actual grace is a transient action, a motion intended to spur on the will of man, whereas habitual grace clothes the soul in a permanent habit or disposition. We can likewise define actual grace as a supernatural, divine influence upon the soul, which God imparts by way of a transient action, in order to move the soul towards the achievement of a supernatural end.[119]

The Council of Trent's Decree on Justification also makes reference to the role of actual grace. Jesus Christ continuously infuses strength into the justified as does the vine into the branches (see Jn 15:1–8): "This strength always precedes, accompanies, and follows their good works, which, without it, could in no way be pleasing to God and meritorious."[120] This actual grace is absolutely necessary for pursuing all salvific acts,[121] for as our Lord says, "Without

---

[118] Ibid.

[119] Cf. Sylvester J. Hunter, SJ, *Outlines of Dogmatic Theology*, vol. 3 (London: Longmans Green & Co, 1900), 21; Ludwig Ott, *Fundamentals of Catholic Dogma* (Rockford, Illinois: TAN Books, 1974), 225.

[120] DH 1546.

[121] Cf. DH 1552. This doctrine about the absolute necessity of actual grace was laid down ever since the Second Synod of Orange (529):

me you can do nothing" (Jn 15:5), as regards this most necessary supernatural aid. The necessity of actual grace touches even those in the state of sin, contrary to those who have incorrectly asserted that all actions of sinners are sinful. It is true that man can come to know the truth on the natural level without any supernatural light and accomplish good actions, for his nature is not corrupted. Nonetheless, divine grace is still necessary for all men, whether it be in the natural order—to do good and to persevere in it—or, much more, in the supernatural order.

Divisions of Actual Grace

With regard to actual grace, St. Augustine[122] expressly teaches that God *prepares* the will of man to perform good works. When man consequently begins to cooperate with this initial divine movement, God, with His operation, proceeds to *perfect* what He has begun. God, who initiates the good we will to perform, cooperates with our will in the completion of the act, that we may perform it perfectly. From this, I will draw a first distinction: grace is *operative* when it precedes the

---

see DH 377 and 397 (conclusion on grace, human cooperation and predestination by St. Caesarius of Arles), even if its major development began after the sixteenth century. The fifteenth Synod of Carthage (418) had condemned those who held that grace was given only to facilitate the observance of God's Ten Commandments, as if free will would have been able to do this, even if grace were not given, though not as easily, DH 228. Behind this error there was Pelagius, who reduced grace to a good moral example.

[122] St. Augustine, *De gratia et libero arbitrio*, lib. 1, c. 17, n. 33.

human act and functions as the source of that meritorious action, enabling man to initiate a good work; whereas grace is *cooperative* when it operates as the principle of a meritorious action, accompanying the human act already begun.

Moreover, the grace that comes at an early stage is said to *stir*, as its work is to awaken a man's life and to dispose him to God. When a person is thus awakened and proceeds to act, grace will *help* him to perform the work. The grace that assists man is *prevenient*—coming from the Latin *praevenient*, "coming before"—as it precedes all action, or it is *subsequent*, when it follows the action. Grace is always one and indivisible; all these distinctions are to be made when we consider the chronological narrative of grace's operation in the lives of men.

Actual grace brings about different effects on man's life. Its overall and continuous effect is laid down by St. Thomas in the following way: "The healing of the soul, willing the good, doing the good efficaciously, persevering in the good, reaching glory."[123] The grace that initiates the actualization of these effects is considered to be *prevenient*, with respect to the realization of the effect that follows; the grace that actually produces the effect is considered *subsequent* with respect to the former (the prevenient grace). The narrative of divine grace will cease when man has reached eternal glory, which is nothing other than the completion of grace and grace itself, as we will see shortly.

---

[123] *ST* I-II, Q. 111, art. 3. Here St. Thomas follows closely St. Augustine, *De natura et gratia*, c. 31.

We shall outline one last distinction of grace: *external* grace and *internal* grace. External grace is that which affects man's life from without, as, for example and above all, the mystery of the Incarnation, the preaching of the Holy Gospel, the blessing of being born in a Christian country, etc. Internal grace is that which immediately affects the soul. Internal grace, or "created grace," is that which we know as sanctifying grace and actual grace—those graces which act upon the soul either with a permanent, adhesive action, or as transient motions.[124] Internal grace has the priority and is the goal of Christian life. In fact, external grace is oriented towards man's participation by grace in the divine nature.

Grace Perfects Human Nature

In this pathway of discovering the beauty of divine grace and its operation within ourselves, we have come to understand that grace is a divine creation and a supernatural action. It always enjoys precedence over human nature, raising it up to a supernatural status without ever undermining or annulling it. Grace is God's creation and man's participation in the inner life of God. Yet grace works gently to perfect nature. In dealing with this intimate relationship between nature and grace, we observe no mixture between the two, but only a harmonious cooperation: nature is the very foundation of the working of grace in man, and grace is the perfection of his human nature.

---

[124] Cf. Hunter, *Outlines of Dogmatic Theology*, 9–16; Ott, *Fundamentals*, 220–22.

Without human nature in need of healing and elevation towards God, grace would be unnecessary, for nothing would need perfecting. This clearly shows that grace
does require nature and cannot be a substitute for it—the
supernatural never replaces the natural. Without grace,
human nature cannot conform itself to God and reach the
beatific vision of Him. Therefore, the natural finds its inner
fulfilment and perfection in the supernatural, even though
the two are distinct from each other.

In the interrelationship between the natural order and
the supernatural order, on the one hand, we must hold firm
to the transcendence of the supernatural, to exclude any
possible exigency on account of the creature. Nature, in
turn, does not need grace to subsist, because grace, which
is freely given by God, far surpasses the limits of man's
expectations. On the other hand, we should keep in mind
that the supernatural roots itself into nature, and in so doing, perfects nature. While we stick to the distinction of
the two orders—the natural and the supernatural—with
the Magisterium of the Church,[125] we affirm the intimate
harmony existing between nature and grace, reason and
faith, grace and freedom.

St. Thomas Aquinas, in studying the meaning of sacred
doctrine, i.e., theology as a true science, insofar as it draws
its principles of argumentation (the articles of faith) from
the Authority of God, demonstrates that sacred doctrine

---

[125] See Council of Trent, *Decree on Justification*, can. 4: DH 1554;
First Vatican Council, *Dei Filius*, c. 4: DH 3017–19.

makes use of reason and does not reject it, not in order to prove the truths of the faith, but to explain the things proposed therein. By arguing thus, Aquinas states his well-known teaching, which is a compendium of what we are saying: "*Since therefore grace does not destroy nature but perfects it*, natural reason should minister to faith as the natural bent of the will ministers to charity."[126]

Logically, the following questions arise: how can nature be opened to the supernatural and thus to the activity of divine grace? Is it possible for a man to begin to long for grace and then receive it? How can reason minister to faith?

We can answer these questions, keeping in mind that the relation between grace and nature is the relation between a perfection (grace) and the perfectible (rational or intellectual nature). Nature cannot be wholly closed to the supernatural because the same Author has made both. Here we recall the beautiful text of Isaiah 54:5, which essentially states that the Creator is our Redeemer. There exists, therefore, an openness of human nature—a natural capacity to receive grace and to welcome it as a divine gift. This natural openness to grace has been defined by theologians as *potentia obedientialis* or obediential power: a capability or capacity for obeying God.

This *potentia obedientialis* is man's capability to receive supernatural goods from God and to make use of them. On their own natural strength, humans cannot enjoy

---

[126] *ST* I, Q. 1, art. 8, ad 2, emphasis added.

God's beatific vision and see Him face to face unless God makes it possible by conferring on human nature the gift of grace. This gift can be received because nature is open to God, for man, with his intellect, can know God, and with his will desire Him.[127] This power to obey God, being naturally inclined to Him, is rooted in this capability of human nature. It is a natural power, not only *passive* in regard to the supernatural good to be received, but also *active*, in the sense that, enabled by grace, man responds to God.

Moreover, this capability to obey God, carved into nature, is characterized by two qualities, one metaphysical and the other psychological (as regards the human soul). The former is expressed by human intelligence's power to know God as a true and existing Being. Man is open to God as *Primum Principium*—the First Principle of all things. The latter is characterized by a dynamism of the human will to move towards the very goal of all happiness and love: this is the *natural desire* for God. Humans, by their intellect and will, are receptive to God and can potentially obey Him. This potential of human nature is satisfied and brought to completion when God reveals Himself and gives His divine grace. We may sum up by saying that man is capable of God because *"naturaliter anima est capax gratiae"*—"the soul is naturally capable of grace." Furthermore, as the soul

---

[127] It is already St. Augustine who speaks of this potential of human nature, although he does not use this terminology. See *De praedestinatione Sanctorum*, 5, 10.

is made in the likeness of God, it is fitting that it receives God by grace.[128]

The natural desire to see God is truly effective in understanding this intimate bond between nature and grace and their reciprocal relationship. With Blessed John Duns Scotus, we may say that God is the natural goal of man and his happiness, but this goal is not achievable outside of divine grace, that is, without a supernatural intervention from God. This desire for God is a *pondus*—a weight pushing human will towards this supernatural end. This capability of elevation towards the supernatural order by grace is more than an ability to obey: it is a power engraved by God into human nature. Henceforth, humans have a natural inclination to faith and charity, for human nature has been endowed by God with a natural inclination to perfection.[129] This natural inclination is very much evident in the natural desire to see God. In every man there lies a longing for God. However, this desire cannot be ultimately pursued outside of grace. For Duns Scotus, the *potentia obedientialis* is a power in man's possession ordered passively to a greater perfection—the perfection of finally knowing God and of having life in Him. For this reason, the perfection of intelligent beings can only be wrought by a supernatural agent—God.[130] This definitively shows

---

[128] *ST* I-II, Q. 113, art. 10.

[129] Bl. John Duns Scotus, *Quaestiones in IV libros Sententiarum*, Prologus, Q. 1, n. 23.

[130] Scotus, *Ordinatio*, Prologus, part I, n. 94.

the inner link between nature and grace: in between, the human will plays the role of bridge.

Grace and Glory

The ultimate goal of divine grace is the beatific vision of God, that "face-to-face" vision by which one sees God "as He really is" (1 Jn 3:2). In fact, St. Paul says: "Now we are seeing a dim reflection in a mirror; but then we shall be seeing face to face. The knowledge that I have now is imperfect; but then I shall know as fully as I am know" (1 Cor 13:12). Grace has its completion in this vision, in the glory of God. This means that the purpose of grace is eschatological, transcendent: "Those whom he justified he also glorified" (Rom 8:30). The grace-giving process—the justification of a sinner and his transformation into a child of God—has this ultimate goal: the glorification of a person in Christ, to be there, where our Lord has preceded us. God has predestined us to this glory; hence, glory is "consummated grace,"[131] its final destination.

On this point, all the great medieval theologians concur. For St. Thomas, "grace and glory are referred to the same genus, for grace is nothing other than a beginning of glory in us."[132] The Latin word that expresses this beginning is *inchoatio*. Grace is "*inchoatio gloriae*": by grace, we already possess the glorification that will be fully revealed in us in heaven. We can also say, with St. Elizabeth of the

---

[131] St. Thomas, *De Veritate*, Q. 27, art. 2, ad 7.
[132] *ST* II-II, Q. 24, art. 3, ad 2.

Trinity, that grace is the presence of heaven within us. For St. Bonaventure, the grace that sanctifies us and the glory of heaven are both a divine influence on the soul, through which a human soul possesses God and God abides in the soul.[133] Finally, Scotus adds that grace is really identical with glory, that is, by its nature, grace is a disposition to it.[134] All graces lead to glory, but strictly speaking, sanctifying grace is the necessary and immediate means to it.

With a poignant expression of O'Callaghan, we say that glory is "grace at home."[135] This Irish theologian also adds the following:

> The eschatological purpose of Christian grace in glory allows us to appreciate two fundamental and inseparable aspects of grace itself: its realism and its hidden or enigmatic character. In effect, the life of the Christian is "hidden with Christ in God" (Col 3:3). It is marked by what we might call an "eschatological reserve:" it is situated in the human space, but the latter is open to development, to growth in the interiorizing of faith, of hope, and of charity, and it is marked by the *chiaroscuro* of history and human freedom.[136]

Grace is not a metaphor, but a great dynamic reality, transforming a person into a new entity: the sinner becomes

---

[133] St. Bonaventure, *In II Sententiarum*, Dist. 27, art. 1, q. 3.

[134] Bl. John Duns Scotus, *Ordinatio*, Bk. 4, Dist. 1, Q. 1.

[135] O'Callaghan, *God Ahead of Us*, 131.

[136] Ibid.

a child of God, adopted by grace. Glory, as the supreme destiny of Christian life, shows forth God's true desire for us to become sharers of His divinity in a process of continuous transformation; this is pointed out by St. Paul as a transformation into the image of Christ, "from glory to glory, as by the Spirit of the Lord" (2 Cor 3:18). Grace is, indeed, this transformation into Christ, embodying the mystical aspect of Christian life, until its full consummation in glory. Here again we see the harmonious passage from ascetical to mystical life.

Reflecting on the meaning of glory, we come to understand that Christian life is a new life, a life sanctified in Christ. From the very first moment of sanctification by justification, the Christian has the duty of carrying out this important commitment: to be holy and spotless in God's presence through love (see Eph 1:4). Christian sanctification is not something extrinsic or a mere ideal. On the contrary, it defines, in fact, what a Christian *is* and his call to sanctity. Holiness pertains to the very essence of Christian life.

Can Grace Be Experienced?

Let us now deal with grace in relation to our way of knowing things. Is there any perception of grace, any way to be aware of its presence within us? Can we know whether we are in the state of grace? We leave aside for our purposes the experiences of mystics and especially that rare privilege a few saints have received, namely, "confirmation in grace": a way to know for sure, while still on this earth, that salvation and eternal glory will be infallibly achieved.[137] This is an extraordinary grace, as happened to St. Paul (see 2 Cor 12:9), which is to be counted among the graces *gratis datae*—graces that are *charisms*, to be distinguished from graces *gratum faciens*—graces that render a person pleasing to God through actual and sanctifying grace.

The Council of Trent, in order to oppose the Lutheran errors of a subjective fideism, clearly states that there is no knowledge of one's state of grace.[138] Ordinarily, one cannot have an infallible certainty about one's personal state of grace, but only a practical, or better yet, moral certitude that one is living in the state of grace. According to St. Thomas Aquinas, one may morally be sure of possessing habitual or sanctifying grace if the heart is filled and satisfied with the things of God. In other words, I may be sure if I am conscious of delighting in God and despising worldly things by seeing them as subordinated to God, and inasmuch as I am unconscious of any mortal sin.[139] Another moral indication of the presence of grace, given by St. Francis de Sales, is one's having a profound devotion to our Lady, as an insurance to persevere in grace, since Mary our Mother intercedes for her children.[140]

With all these signs we might recognize in our daily Christian life, we can speak of an "experience of grace,"

---

[137] This is what St. Thomas calls the knowledge of grace by revelation: *ST* I-II, Q. 112, art. 5.

[138] Cf. DH 1533; 1536.

[139] Ibid.

[140] Cf. Journet, *Meaning of Grace*, 77.

but only by faith, and only in the realm of this theological virtue. We cannot ever presume to be in the state of grace, but by praying and detaching ourselves from all mortal sin, we can draw nearer to God, with confidence and filial fear.

The Grace of the Holy Spirit

Continuing our investigation, we now examine a new aspect of grace: its specific relation with the Holy Spirit. Grace is a divine and supernatural gift, enabling a person to share in God's divine nature and consequently to be in relation with the Father, the Son, and the Holy Spirit—the Triune God. We ask now the following question: does the Holy Spirit have a particular role in the sanctification of souls, or is this role to be attributed to all three Persons, inasmuch as they act together *ad extra*—outside their inner mystery, in the history of salvation?

More precisely: even as the work of the Incarnation, wrought by all three Persons of the Holy Trinity, is attributed especially to the Second Person, the Word made flesh—as protagonist and terminal point—may we likewise attribute the work of sanctification, common to all three divine Persons, to the Holy Spirit, the Sanctifier? Can we push ourselves to the point of establishing a possible analogy: that as the Word became flesh and dwelt amongst us in the humanity of Christ, so the Holy Spirit, through grace, inhabits the soul in grace and is personally present in it? Obviously, we speak not of identity, but of similarity.

It is fitting to begin with St. Bonaventure—a Franciscan Doctor of the Church—who is keen on referring to divine grace as the "grace of the Holy Spirit."[141] He asserts: "Grace is a gift bestowed and infused directly by God. For truly, together with grace and by means of grace, we receive the Holy Spirit, the uncreated Gift, the good and perfect Gift *coming down from the Father of Lights* through the Word made flesh . . ."[142] St. Bonaventure, in a significant way, here affirms that with created grace and by it, we receive the uncreated grace, the Holy Spirit. It is important, however, always to have in mind that the only possible way to receive the Holy Spirit is through the gift of grace; otherwise, we would be saying that we could be transformed into God Himself and thus fall into pantheism. St. Thomas Aquinas, reading from the same page, affirms: "By the gift of sanctifying grace the rational creature is perfected so that it can freely use not only the created gift itself, but enjoy also the divine person Himself; and so the invisible mission takes place according to the gift of sanctifying grace; and yet the divine person Himself is given."[143]

---

[141] This is the title of the section of his *Breviloquium* dedicated to divine grace.

[142] St. Bonaventure, *Breviloquium*, part V, c. 1, n. 2.

[143] St. Thomas, *ST* I, Q. 43, art. 3, ad 1. Also his reply to objection 2 (same question and article) is significant: "Sanctifying grace disposes the soul to possess the divine person; and this is signified when it is said that the Holy Ghost is given according to the gift of grace. Nevertheless the gift itself of grace is from the Holy Ghost; which is signified by the words, the charity of God is poured forth in our hearts by the Holy Ghost.'"

In the development of the doctrine of grace, Matthias Joseph Scheeben—one of the most important theologians of the twentieth century—argues that, according to the Fathers of the Church, the Holy Spirit is usually designated as the divine Person to whom we are united through grace, for the distribution of divine grace pertains to Him. For this reason, the union of God with the creature and of the creature with God is attributed to the Holy Spirit, especially since He is the personal expression of divine love. On the one hand, God's union with the creature is effected through His love; on the other hand, our union with God in this life is shown especially by our love for God. Love, then, is the lynchpin, for it manifests the work of grace in us.[144]

Scheeben continues his argument, arriving at the crux of the matter:

> Thus following the Fathers and the theologians, it would be against faith to hold that the divine Spirit is in us by reason of His gifts only, and not by His very being. Accordingly, we must believe that He gives Himself to us with His gifts, from which He is inseparable. St. Augustine does not hesitate to affirm that the Holy Ghost is His own gift. Theology has, as a result, given to the Holy Ghost the name "Gift" as a proper designation of Him.[145]

---

[144] Matthias Joseph Scheeben, *The Glories of Dvine Grace: A Fervent Exhortation to All to Preserve and to Grow in Sanctifying Grace* (Rockford, Illinois: TAN Books, 2000), 71.

[145] Ibid., 71–72.

In his explication of the personal presence of the Holy Spirit in body and soul, Scheeben refers to numerous scriptural passages to support his argument: the inhabitation of the Holy Spirit even in the flesh, thus becoming His temple (cf. 1 Cor 6:18); the person in grace, who is transformed by the power of the Spirit of God into the image of God (2 Cor 3:18); the pouring forth of the charity of God—that highest love, which is of the essence of God—into our hearts by the Holy Spirit, who is given to us (Rom 5:5; note again, how evident is the link between charity and the Holy Spirit); the reception of the Spirit of Truth, promised by our Lord, that He may *remain* with us (Jn 14:16). Scheeben draws a splendid conclusion: "In a twofold way and for a twofold reason, we are really and truly united with the Holy Ghost through grace. First, insofar as He, the source of grace, comes to us with it and unites Himself with us: and again, insofar as grace leads us to Him and unites us with Him."[146]

Grace and Charity

Having broadened our understanding of the personal presence of the Holy Spirit in us by sanctifying grace, we reiterate that the Holy Spirit is the Sanctifier who gives us divine grace, and the one who abides in us by grace. But another question here arises, most surely a consequence of the former one: what is the relationship between grace and love, or more precisely, between grace and charity, since this last is the highest love and the essence of God—"charity is of

---

[146] Ibid., 73–74.

God" and "God is charity" (1 Jn 4:7, 4:16)? This point aims at finding out the precise manner of coordinating grace, love, and the personal action of the Holy Spirit.

This question was initially outlined by the Master of the *Sentences*, Peter Lombard, who was keen on simply identifying the Holy Spirit with the virtue of charity. Inspired by St. Augustine, he writes that "the Holy Spirit Himself is the love or the charity with which we love God and our neighbor."[147] This sentence, though inspiring, must be correctly understood. We cannot assume from this that the Holy Spirit absorbs into Himself the human action of loving God, so that a confusion or mixing of persons might emerge. It can only be understood in the same way as that in which St. Augustine spoke of the love of God that is poured forth into our hearts insofar as God in the Holy Spirit makes us lovable and capable of loving Him—"*facit nos dilectores suos*."[148]

Put simply, created grace, as already mentioned, cannot be ignored in our present consideration. The Holy Spirit makes His abode within us only through this created entity, by being present personally and making us capable of loving God. "By grace, in fact, humans are rendered lovable; they become children of God. Augustine says as much: "Because you have loved me, you have made me lovable.""[149] The starting point for delving into the intimate depths of

---

[147] Peter Lombard, *I Sententiarum*, Dist. 17, art. 1.

[148] St. Augustine, *De spiritu et littera*, 32.56.

[149] O'Callaghan, *God Ahead of Us*, 71.

God's mystery is sanctifying grace. The Holy Spirit indeed is within us—but never apart from the habit of sanctification and regeneration. We can "posses" the Spirit of God if we live in grace according to this Spirit.

Nonetheless, can we enter more profoundly into the relationship between grace and love? Is there a real distinction between the two, as St. Thomas affirms, or is it merely a question of a formal distinction, as Duns Scotus prefers to say, the two being the one same thing? For Aquinas, grace is objectively distinct from charity, for whereas the former is a *habitus*, the latter is a theological and operative virtue, presupposing a divine status of the soul in order to operate. Charity presupposes the soul's elevation to the state of grace; thus, they are two different entities. Here is the text of Aquinas:

> It is written in the Epistle to the Romans (5:5): "The charity of God is poured forth in our hearts, by the Holy Ghost who is given to us." Then the giving of the Holy Ghost precedes charity as a cause its effect. But the Holy Ghost is given to us as a result of a particular gift of His. Then there is a particular gift in us which precedes charity, and this does not seem to be anything but grace. Consequently grace is something other than charity.[150]

---

[150] St. Thomas, *De Veritate*, Q. 27, art. 2. For Thomists, the human will is an appetite of the intellect, which means that the intellectual knowledge must choose accordingly; the same holds for charity, which follows the virtue of faith, given by grace.

In contrast, Duns Scotus speaks of habitual grace as something truly identical with the virtue of charity supernaturally infused. Thus, all perfections that we may attribute to the one may also be attributed to the other. If they were really distinct from one another, either of the two would be superfluous, inasmuch as the other would suffice.[151] Hence, man could be saved either with the one or with the other.[152] Here is his principal thought on the identity of grace and charity:

> Charity is defined as such insofar as the one who possesses it holds God as a dear person, so that he can look at God not as He is loving the creature but inasmuch as He is lovable. Grace is that entity through which the one who possesses it is well accepted in God's sight, so that grace refers to God as the One who accepts and loves, not insofar as he is loved.[153]

Therefore, if grace were charity, this last would precede faith. Alternatively, in the theology of Duns Scotus, human will does not *necessarily* follow the intellect but it does *freely*, in the sense that it might also choose not to assent to the truth presented to it by intellectual knowledge. So charity does not necessarily follow faith; it might also precede it, since it is the prerogative of God, bestowed on Christians through grace, together with faith and hope. This is because, as we will now discuss, for Scotus, grace is identical with charity and only formally distinct from it.

[151] Bl. John Duns Scotus, *Ordinatio*, Bk. 2, Dist. 27, q. un.

[152] Scotus, *Reportationes Parisienses*, Bk. 2, Dist. 27, n. 3.

[153] Scotus, *Ordinatio*, Bk. 2, Dist. 27, q. un.

Expressed simply, for Scotus, the formal difference between grace and charity, objectively identical, consists in this: charity is that by which I love God, grace is that by which God loves me. From a person's point of view, charity is the formal active aspect, while grace is the passive formal aspect of one supernatural entity. Without a doubt, the question is subtle but equally inspiring. If grace is truly love and both identically the same, then the Holy Spirit abides in me by His love. The love of God that makes me lovable is due to the personal presence of the Holy Spirit in me. In this way, the words of St. John become indeed clear: "every one that loves is born of God and knows God" (1 Jn 4:7). And again, John 14:23, which reads thus: "If any one love me, he will keep my word. And my Father will love him and we will come to him and will make our abode with him." Here love effects the inhabitation of the Holy Trinity in the soul of the lover. The indwelling presence of God is a permanent effect in the soul, which lasts as long as sanctifying grace is kept. It is only grace that makes God present and thus reproduces in the soul, by participation, the Trinitarian relationships of *generation* between the Father and the Son, and of the *spiration* of the Holy Spirit from the Father with the Son. It seems, however, that love attracts God into the soul, while grace keeps Him as a most dear inhabitant.

The Council of Trent did not intervene formally on this question, although it anathematized those who held the position that men are justified either by the imputation of Christ's justice alone or by the remission of sins alone, "excluding [the] grace and charity that is poured into their hearts by the Holy Spirit (cf. Rm 5:5)."[154] At first glance, it seems that the mind of Trent is to differentiate grace and charity, even if, according to St. Robert Bellarmine, the Council has rather favored the identity of grace and charity.[155]

Dogmatically speaking, we are not bound to believe one option over the other, though it is well worth noting the depths of a dogmatic question. One thing is beyond doubt: the mystery of grace is crucially central to the supernatural organism such that only through its operation may we access God's infinite love for us and truly become His abode in this world. Grace and love are interdependent. We do not lose faith and hope through mortal sin, but we do lose charity, because we lose sanctifying grace. Charity can be alive in us only together with grace. The faith and hope that still remain in a soul caught up in mortal sin are "not formed," and therefore, truly imperfect, for, without grace and love, we cannot merit eternal life.

As St. Augustine says, "*fides bene operari non potest, nisi per dilectionem*"—"faith cannot operate well except through love,"[156] commenting on the words of St. Paul: "what matters is faith that works by charity" (Gal 5:6). The faith and hope that remain in the absence of grace and charity *do*, however, lead a sinner to return to God through regaining the state of sanctifying grace, ordinarily with

---

[154] DH 1561.

[155] St. Robert Bellarmine, *De gratia et libero arbitrio*, Bk. 1, cc. 6–7.

[156] St. Augustine, *Sermo* 156, 5, 5.

sacramental confession or extraordinarily with an act of perfect contrition.

In conclusion, the profound unity of divine grace and divine love leads us to see that with the outpouring of divine love in us, we have God the Holy Spirit present within us through divine grace. It is fitting to allow Scheeben a final word on this issue:

> When God gives us faith and hope, He does not come Himself but merely sends His gifts, that they may prepare a place for Him. But when love is poured out into our hearts, the Holy Ghost Himself is given to us. He comes to us with grace to dwell in our souls. This supernatural love is, therefore, as great a gift as grace itself; indeed, according to the opinion of St. Augustine, even as great as the Holy Ghost Himself, who through it and in it is given to us.[157]

---

[157] Scheeben, *Glories of Divine Grace*, 203. Cf. St. Augustine, *Sermo* 156, 5, 5; *Epistola* 186, 2, 4; 3, 7.

5

Two Emblematic Positions on Grace, Both Heterodox

IN THE TWENTIETH CENTURY, THEOLOGICAL reflection on grace has seen a renewed interest among theologians. There has been an effort to readdress the classic view on nature and grace in order to overcome a sort of dichotomy between the two, which has been defined as *extrinsicism*. With what results? We concentrate here on two important theological attempts, inspired by the method of the so-called *nouvelle théologie*, both very central in the theological panorama in preparation of Vatican II, playing also a pivotal role in its aftermath. It is worth studying these two positions for the many consequences that both enfold, and for their impact on the proclamation of the faith in today's world. The authors that we will now examine are two Jesuit priests, the French Henri de Lubac (1896–1991) and the German Karl Rahner (1904–1984).

Their positions are different, but still two sides of the same coin. For example, Rahner does not accept de Lubac's theory that human nature is intrinsically oriented toward grace and the beatific vision. In de Lubac's understanding of the necessity of grace in the order of creation, there are two central elements:[158] he refuses the concept of "pure nature" and believes that the natural desire to see God is not *de facto* natural but already supernatural, since God cannot cease from enkindling it in our nature. It is rendering the human nature supernatural *per se* by building an exigence of the supernatural into the creature. And yet, in Rahner's attempt to distinguish more clearly between nature and grace, he binds the two in an existential way, creating *ex novo* a "supernatural existential," which is at once natural (because human knowledge lies open to the infinite horizon of being as existence) and supernatural (insofar as this infinite horizon of being, in disclosing all the breadth of being, is God Himself, reached in transcendental experience). This will lead, albeit only gradually, to "naturalized" grace. Let us now study these two theories in greater depth.

Henri de Lubac: Grace Comes with Nature

A very influential philosopher of the *nouvelle théologie* movement, Maurice Blondel (1851–1949), proposed a drastic change of perspective in regard to the classic understanding of nature open to grace and grace as perfecting nature. Particularly significant was his work *L'Action* (1893), in

---

[158] For a critical evaluation of his position, see Guy Mansini, "Henri de Lubac, the Natural Desire to See God and Pure Nature," in *Gregorianum* 83.1 (2002): 89–109, and on the theological importance of the pure nature, A.-M. Léonard, "La nécessité théologique du concept de nature pure," in *Revue Thomiste* 109 (2001): 345–51.

which he addressed the risk of a divine and supernatural Revelation becoming totally extrinsic to man if understood merely as a gift "from above," on a level completely separated from nature. For Blondel, nature and grace, and therefore the capacity of man to respond to a supernatural Revelation, are not on two different levels. They are rather intrinsic to human action, which can achieve its goal only through supernatural Revelation. From here, Blondel draws the conclusion that there is an "exigence" and even a "necessity" for man to receive grace, rejecting what he sees as the "extrinsicism" of (neo-)scholastics who maintain there are external signs, such as miracles, given as rational aids to belief. He formulates a paradox concerning the reality of grace, absolutely impossible to man's enterprise, yet absolutely necessary to him: "*Absolument impossibile et absolument necessaire à l'homme, c'est là proprement la notion du surnaturel.*"[159] The ban on anything coming from outside man's conscience in order to move him to believe was incorrect and dangerously verging on immanentism. In fact, as for sanctifying grace, so for supernatural Revelation: the necessary supernatural illumination of man's intelligence, as well as its elevation to a superior order, does not come from inside the conscience of man, but from above, from God.

And so, with Blondel, a "principle of immanence" was formulated. It became very influential on some theologians, such as our French Jesuit, although received through the philosophical mediation of two other Jesuits: Pierre

---

[159] Maurice Blondel, *L'Action* (Paris: Alcan, 1893), 388.

Rousselot (1878–1915) and Joseph Maréchal (1878–1944), who both tried to integrate German Idealism into systematic philosophy, opening up the concept of transcendental knowledge (according to the categories of Immanuel Kant) as "relation with God." This will be very influential particularly in both Rahner and de Lubac's understanding of grace.

De Lubac's principal thesis was formulated in his renowned work *Surnaturel* (1946), more developed and updated in successive works, especially in *Le mystère du surnaturel* (1965).[160] As already mentioned, he rejects the concept of "pure nature," namely, the hypothesis of a nature created not in grace and with no necessity of a beatific vision. It is strictly a theological hypothesis because a "pure nature" does not exist in reality, since nature was created and elevated in grace, lost afterwards in the Fall. Nevertheless, it is a useful theological concept to help explain nature and grace. St. Augustine had already raised the question:[161] could God create human nature in the same condition in which it found itself after falling into sin? The answer was that God certainly could. So nature was not *per se* and of necessity oriented to grace; grace was freely given. The classic position, as previously seen, is that grace was originally given to nature as an infused gift from God (extrinsically), but, at the same time, nature was created to long for God's vision (an

---

[160] For an English version, see Henri de Lubac, *The Mystery of the Supernatural* (New York: Herder & Herder, 1998).

[161] See St. Augustine, *De libero arbitrio*, III, 20, 56 and *Retractationes*, I, 9, 6.

intrinsic *desiderium naturale videndi Deum*: a natural desire to see God).[162] The bond between God's gift and human desire has been labelled, as already discussed, *potentia obedientialis*, i.e., the capacity of human nature to obey God and to be led into union with His divine nature.

De Lubac insisted that the hypothesis of a pure nature causes a separation between God and the world for those living in the modern world, between a world without God and a Christianity estranged from the world. He firmly rejected any hypothesis of a pure nature. In 1950, Pius XII intervened with the Encyclical Letter *Humani Generis*, in which he rejected the error of immanentism and defended the theoretical possibility of a pure nature and the non-necessary call of man to a beatific vision.[163] As a result of this, Father de Lubac, together with some other Jesuits, was removed from his teaching post.

According to de Lubac, the natural desire to see God is absolute and not conditional, meaning that it does not

---

[162] See for example St. Thomas, *ST* I, Q. 12, art. 1; I, Q. 75, art. 6 ; *Summa contra Gentiles* III, c. 57.

[163] DH 3891: "Others destroy the gratuity of the supernatural order, since God, they say, cannot create intellectual beings without ordering and calling them to the beatific vision." Cf. CCC 367: "Sometimes the soul is distinguished from the spirit: St. Paul for instance prays that God may sanctify his people 'wholly,' with 'spirit and soul and body' kept sound and blameless at the Lord's coming. The Church teaches that this distinction does not introduce a duality into the soul. 'Spirit' signifies that from creation man is ordered to a supernatural end and that his soul can gratuitously be raised beyond all it deserves to communion with God."

depend on whether or not God is willing to give it to me. To the "absolute desire" would correspond a completion or fulfillment that is not, strictly speaking, owed or due to it. Hence, for our French Jesuit, there is *only one end in man and this is a necessarily supernatural end.* In other words, grace is due to human nature necessarily, with no possibility of a creation without grace and without supernatural Revelation. There is no longer that indispensable distinction, classically highlighted, between a natural beatitude and a supernatural goal as God's free gift.

What is the alarming consequence of this alternative perspective on nature and grace? Despite all good intentions of bringing human society back to God and Christianity back into society, the very crux of the matter here is a "supernaturalization" of human nature. According to de Lubac, in fact, "God's call is *constitutive* of the nature,"[164] even if the concept of "nature" was never properly defined. There would only be one supernatural world, inclusive of some human elements such as human nature, the faculties of the soul, etc. Consequently, there is no longer a legitimate autonomy of human reason and philosophical reflection, as well as no distinction between nature and grace. If this were the case, an unavoidable question arises: what is nature, and what is grace? The two, if not distinguished, are mixed one into the other and so confused, to the point of missing the

---

[164] Henri de Lubac, *Mystère du surnaturel* (Paris: Aubier, 1965), 81. See also idem, *Mémoire sur l'occasion de mes écrits* (Namur: Culture et Vérité, 1989), 65.

importance of each, with a fatal loss of the infinite value of grace. In this framework of thought, the supernatural as such can no longer be identified, as its distinction (logical and metaphysical) from human nature does not exist anymore. This is also truly harmful for civil life, because, rather than bringing State and Church back into harmony, it may provoke their final farewell. If grace comes with nature, why should we try to seek it out? And if the beatific vision is a necessity of nature, could someone choose to renounce it? Salvation, indeed faith and Christian life in its entirety, may come to be seen as a right rather than a gift, and the possibility of eternal perdition may come to be excluded. Today's culture is so permeated with the desire for rights at any cost, it would no longer be challenged by a theology of grace that seems not to ask for deeper conversion. Though diametrically opposed, this way of reasoning would match a second attempt to make grace more relevant and less "extrinsic," but *de facto* naturalizing it: the theory of Karl Rahner.

Karl Rahner: Grace Is in Nature as Nature Is Necessarily Open to Grace

The theological reflection of the German Jesuit Karl Rahner is far more complicated than that of de Lubac. It is a constant intersection of philosophy and theology, resulting in a transcendental Thomism[165] that welds together being, knowledge,

---

[165] That is, St. Thomas read with the lens of Joseph Marechal through the Kantian categories of knowledge, where the subject fundamentally has priority over reality.

and grace. I will dedicate a thorough investigation to this theological system that has so greatly influenced theology in our modern times, particularly the mystery of grace, rewriting with modern/transcendental categories the possibility for man to know God and find salvation.

To understand Rahner it is necessary to start with his philosophical works.[166] The beginnings are seen in the end, but at the same time, they are verified and modified during the process, as is natural in a maturing of thought. One needs to pay attention to his very first philosophical work, *Spirit in the World* (*Geist in Welt*, 1939, presented as a doctoral thesis in philosophy but rejected by his professor), outlining the main trajectories of this investigation. From here, moving through another important work, *Hearer of the Word* (*Hörer des Wortes*, 1941) one can easily see the theological development of his thought, culminating in the *Foundations of Christian Faith: An Introduction to the Idea of Christianity* (*Grundkurs des Glaubens: Einführung in den Begriff des Christentums*, 1976), which is a synthesis of Rahner's thought and a new theological architecture, as boasted by J. B. Metz.

---

[166] On the problems opened by Karl Rahner's philosophical and theological thought, see C. Fabro, *La svolta antropologica di Karl Rahner* (Milano: Rusconi, 1974); S. M. Lanzetta (ed.), *Karl Rahner. Un'analisi critica* (Siena: Cantagalli, 2009); G. Cavalcoli, *Karl Rahner. Il Concilio tradito* (Verona: Fede & Cultura, 2009). For a succinct account, see Peter Kwasniewski, "Karl Rahner and the Unspoken Framework of (Much of) Modern Theology," *OnePeterFive*, July 27, 2022, https://onepeterfive.com/karl-rahner-modern-theology/.

In *Spirit in the World*, the word "Spirit" is used to describe not the Holy Spirit but the spirit of man, or better yet,
man as spirit (*Geist*), capable of knowing, and by knowledge,
of laying down the foundation of reality as such. Rahner's
fundamental thesis is the unity of sensibility and intellect:
sense, which in previous classic philosophies seemed passive in relation to the world and dependent on experience,
in reality reveals itself to be internal to the intellect, which
has now become the productive principle of experience.

Experience, above all, is the possibility to know God. It
lays out the problem of God. This, indeed, is at the heart of
Rahner's entire endeavor, and for this reason, he is certainly
admirable. How does he see man's capacity to know God,
so as to come to share in His life? In *Hearers of the Word*,
Rahner says: "God is not a fact that could be grasped by
man and his experience, immediately in his own Self."[167]
Instead, in a lecture on the *Experience of God Today* (*Gottes
Erfahrung heute*), to which Rahner attached great importance by updating it from time to time, he says:

> This experience of God is inevitable. It is indepen-
> dent of whether it is called God or not, whether it
> is conceptually thematised within a theoretical as-
> sertion of God or not, whether man freely identifies

---

[167] "'Gott' keine Tatsache ist, die vom Menschen und seiner Erfahrung unmittelbar in ihrem eigenen Selbst ergriffen werden
könnte," *Hörer des Wortes. Zur Grundlegung einer Religionsphi-
losophie* (Freiburg im Br.: Herder, 1971), 19 (revised by Johannes
Baptist Metz).

with it or opposes it, turns away from it or allows himself to be founded by it. . . . This experience of God is not the privilege of some "mystic," rather it is given in every man, even if the strength and clarity of reflection are very different from it.[168]

This experience of God is "transcendental" (Rahner makes his own the terminology of Kant's gnoseology, meaning a subjective condition for knowing something): it is man's dynamism towards the Absolute, as well as and already towards the Incarnation and the Hypostatic Union.[169] The transcendental experience is also a "transcendental revelation," which becomes concrete or thematic in the Christian Revelation, held as categorical knowledge/revelation. Categorical here stands for thematic, specific, and is opposed to

---

[168] ". . . diese Gotteserfahrung ist unausweichlich. Sie ist davon *unabhängig*, ob man das, worauf sie bezogen ist, Gott nennt oder nicht, ob sie in eine theoretische Aussage von Gott hinein begrifflich thematisiert wird oder nicht, ob der Mensch sich in Freiheit mit ihr identifiziert oder sie ablehnt, verdrängt, auf sie beruhen läßt. . . . Diese Gotteserfahrung ist nicht das Privileg einzelner 'Mystiker,' sonder in jedem Mensch gegeben, wenn auch Kraft und Deutlichkeit der Reflexion auf sie sehr verschieden sind." K. Rahner, *Gotteserfahrung heute* (Freiburg im Breisgau: Herder, 2009), 25.

[169] Cf. Karl Rahner, "Theologie der Menschwerdung," in idem, *Schriften zur Theologie*, vol. IV (1958), 137–55: "Die Menschwerdung Gottes ist daher der einmalig höchste Fall des Wesensvollzugs der menschlichen Wirklichkeit" ("The Incarnation of God is then, in a unique way, the supreme case of the realisation of the essence of human reality").

transcendental, which is an inevitable subjective leaning of
man towards being understood as thought, though still athematic. For Rahner "being and knowledge are the same,"[170]
whereas for classical metaphysics and Christian philosophy
they are necessarily distinct, due to the evidence that there
can be no knowledge without being, on which it depends.

Moreover, this transcendental knowledge of God, which
is divided between what is already given in man and God
who is not merely the *datum* of nature, is welded together
with Rahner's most important self-creation, the "supernatural existential": that original bond of nature and grace, co-
original to man, such as the above-mentioned experience.[171]
Rahner writes:

> This experience [of God] in the concrete situation of
> our existence is to be called both natural and grace-
> formed (*gnadenhaft*), where, however, this support
> of grace (*Gnadenhaftigkeit*) does not mean any sin-
> gular privilege and, on the contrary, the question of

---

[170] Karl Rahner, *Geist in Welt. Zur Metaphysik der endlichen Erkenntnis* (München: Kösel, 1964), 82: "Sein und Erkennen ist dasselbe."

[171] See, in particular, Karl Rahner, *Grundkurs des Glaubens* (Freiburg i.Br: Herder, 1976), 132–39; N. Schwerthfeger, "Der 'anonyme Christ' in der Theologie Karl Rahners," in M. Delgado and M.-L. Bachmann, eds., *Theologie aus Erfahrung der Gnade. An-näherungen an Karl Rahner* (Berlin: Hildesheim, 1994), 72–94; K.-H. Menke, "Existential, übernatürliches," in *LThK³* 3 (1995): 1115; D. Berger, *Natur und Gnade* (Regensburg: Roderer, 1998), 253–322.

the existential acceptance of this experience remains open through freedom.[172]

Here we find the true distinctiveness of Rahner's thought. If, on the one hand, he is praiseworthy for his untiring effort to give God to all men and especially to engage in a dialogue with a deeply secularized Western culture, on the other, it is necessary to point out that this is going too far. Rahner tried to give God to anyone, though subordinating Him to human freedom. For our Jesuit, freedom is the essence of man. Grace is subordinate to freedom too, but in a way that freedom cannot in fact "avoid" it, since it is part of the natural process of experience. This experience is pre-religious and belongs to man as man, being the foundation of any possible spiritual experience. It is the existential opening of one's *Dasein* (being here and now, or also being thrown into existence) which lifts man to the heights of the unreachable mystery.[173] Christianity, says Rahner, is not a bifurcated theory, but a whole, which has something to say to all men insofar as they are men. This "supernatural

---

[172] ". . . in der konkreten Situation unserer Existenz diese Erfahrung 'natürlich' *und* 'gnadenhaft' zugleich nennen, wobei aber diese Gnadenhaftigkeit kein Privileg Einzelner bedeutet und umgekehrt die Frage der existentiellen Annahme dieser Erfahrung in Freiheit durchaus offenbleibt." K. Rahner, *Gotteserfahrung heute*, 27–28.

[173] Cf. ibid., 28; see also the comments of the editor, ibid., 70–71. Cf. also R. Miggelbrink, "Geistliche Erfahrungen sind nicht elitär. Die Theologie Karl Rahners," in *Lebendige Seelsorge* 56 (2005): 317–23, n18.

existential," which is the subjective expression of a "transcendental revelation," is the way to recognize the "anonymous Christians":[174] all men are already touched by grace, even though they are not yet (fully) aware of that. Therefore, all men would already be Christians in a transcendental way, coinciding with the capacity of knowing the infinity of being. In this sense they are "anonymous" and ready to pass from an athematic/transcendental state of Christianity to a thematic/categorical one, by the preaching of the Gospel or by any other grace. Hence, transcendentally speaking, man is already a Christian. According to Rahner, then, salvation for man—including, in particular, for men of the atheistic Western world that has rejected God—is incontrovertibly something that is unavoidable.

The cognitive *a priori* of a Kantian nature that certainly makes use of the data of sensible knowledge, but without which man would not grasp being in its totality—man as spirit ceaselessly asks himself the question about being in its totality, i.e., being which is existence—must be read together with the *Vorgriff*, an *a priori* given to human nature that enables the spirit's dynamic self-awareness of the absolute breadth of all possible knowledge. It is an "advance knowledge" of being in its totality and becomes the true rule of the classic *conversio ad phantasmata*,[175] establishing

---

[174] An expression used by M. Blondel; see Berger, *Natur und Gnade*, 296–300.

[175] Our knowledge starts with our external senses. The internal senses, such as the imagination, are able consequently to work out a first sensible imprinting of that object within ourselves;

the possibility of knowing something and not nothingness. Since man is capable of grasping, "in advance," being in its entirety, he can know being. In truth, we are very close to ontologism, namely, the wrong identification of the *primum logicum* (the apprehension of being in the order of knowledge) with the *primum ontologicum* (being as it is), rather than Thomistic realism.

Now, why can the subject lean towards the infinity of being? Or, what is the (mental) foundation of the infinity of being towards which intelligence extends itself prior to all knowledge? God, Rahner would reply. Yet, evident confusion here lies in identifying being in itself (*esse absolute*) with the absolute Being (*esse absolutum*). Man preemptively grasps God who is the "horizon of transcendence," and through Him grasps the finite. But since God is the *a priori* of knowledge, man is rather "grasped" by God in his cognitive posture. As already said, there is a philosophical assumption of unity between being and knowledge, between the subject of knowledge and the thing known. Rahner identifies the infinity of being/horizon of transcendence with the

---

working on this phantasma, the intellect is finally able to abstract from it the concept and fix it in the intelligence. The *conversio ad phantasmata* of the Scholastic philosophy indicates that human knowledge needs to stick to reality in order to know the truth, whereas with modern philosophy, in particular with Kant, it is rather the knowing subject who, with is innate categories, molds the knowledge of reality. This opens the way to subjectivism, whose effects are visible in some contemporary theologies, more inclined to "narration" than to a systematic presentation of the mystery of faith.

theological notion of God. It brings about a catastrophe in theology, whose reflection is somehow synthesized in an anonymous Christianity, which cannot be understood without the "supernatural existential."

Henceforth, the infinity of mental being would be God, and God would be in man as modifying the knowing subject—not in the sense, however, that man is able to "grasp" God, but in the sense of allowing himself to be grasped by a mystery that is present and always withdrawing. This being present of the existential perception of the infinitude of being is the very content of the "supernatural existential," and it unites indissolubly nature with grace, knowledge with God, albeit mainly in an athematic way, coinciding with existential transcendentalism. What is the conclusion? God is already present in man "athematically" (i.e., without a clear and definite knowledge) as known in the infinite perception of being, which is human existence.

God becomes the existent present in man who discovers himself historically and as a being who can hear the Word. By virtue of this nexus between knower and known, God is already working in man. Although one must move to a categorical knowledge of God by virtue of Revelation, athematically God is already in man, in every man. Rahner justifies his thesis with Vatican II, but merges the implicit knowledge of God (see *Lumen Gentium* 16) with the fact that everyone is already a Christian even if they do not know it. In reality, those who implicitly know God are not already Christians in virtue of their knowledge. There is a natural knowledge of God, explicit or implicit, that precedes the new being of the Christian given to him only by baptism. Certainly, this natural knowledge can become the occasion for baptism, but it is not already the operation of the baptismal effects. It can be baptism of desire or a desire for baptism, but again, it is not already the operation of the grace of the sacrament of baptism, but only of a transient motion, an actual grace, which disposes a person of good will to baptism. In those who are unable to receive baptism but have lived righteously, it is permissible to assume that they would have explicitly desired baptism had they previously known the need for it.[176] In this case, baptism of desire brings about the same effect, eternal salvation, as the sacrament does but without imprinting the character.

Instead, for Rahner, everyone is in grace (habitually/ gnoseologically, even if only anonymously/athematically), whether they know it or not. What is at stake here is the necessity of continuing to preach and baptize. In fact, a crucial question related to the constitutive mission of the Church can be raised. Is there any more a need to evangelize and to still celebrate the sacraments? Rahner would say that it is fitting to do so, since this missionary (traditional) activity would bring knowledge from the transcendental state to the categorical one, but it is not strictly speaking required. For Rahner, salvation is rather given to man as an existential quest. All non-Christians, or the anonymous Christians, are solicited by an innate question about eternal salvation.

---

[176] Cf. CCC 1260.

Again, we must look to identify the definitions of grace and nature. But grace is not nature, and the quest for salvation is not "existential," but rather religious and supernatural. Nature is capable of grace, and this latter comes from above and so perfects nature insofar as nature is capable of grace. The distinction between nature and grace is necessary, but here, in this Rahnerian theological system, there is no room to make distinctions. Where there is no distinction, there is only confusion. The result is that God and man are so indistinguishably united as to dilute God in man, or man in God.

If one delves further into Rahner's theological thought, one realizes that individual actions lose their moral value, their relevance as to good or evil. Rahner drags his distinction between categorical and transcendental into the moral realm too. A moral action is not so much concerned with the objective criterion of its goodness or evil; rather, the moral value of man's actions must be judged by reason of the freedom of the subject, if and to what extent man's freedom is strengthened in his choices. An action that appears thematically wrong would always remain athematically good, as long as it represents an effort to strengthen one's freedom. Hence, it follows that only a thematic choice against God would be a true sin. True sin would be the fundamental negative option. Good and evil would be only subjective, since individual actions are *de facto* deprived of their morality. To them the quality of good and evil does not apply anymore since this would only concern the fundamental option for or against God. At the utmost, human actions can be only "right" or "wrong"—not good or evil. Have we forgotten Rahner's circumlocutions on *Humanae Vitae*, presenting it as part of the non-infallible magisterium?[177] Indeed, the encyclical *Veritatis Splendor* (nn. 65–67) does away with this surreptitious distinction in the moral sphere between categorical and transcendental choice, judging it detrimental to the entire ethical-moral life. The fundamental moral option created by Rahner was thus deprived of any theological standing.

Rahner has been the pioneer in recent times of an anthropocentric turn, riding the wave of Vatican II's anthropological turn. His anthropocentric thought is well manifested in this sentence: "The one who accepts himself completely has accepted the Son of man because in Him God has accepted man."[178] So, to accept oneself is to accept the Son of God. There is nothing more natural than that for Rahner.

A Way Forward: The Classic Distinction and Interdependence of Nature and Grace

Despite their effort to make grace more relevant and to direct people to God in contemporary society, both de Lubac and Rahner have gone too far. De Lubac risks rendering nature into something supernatural, whereas Rahner falls

---

[177] See Rahner's theological reflections on *Humanae Vitae*, in *Stimme der Zeit*, September 1968, reviewed by Card. Avery Dulles in *America*, September 28, 1968.

[178] Rahner, *Grundkurs des Glaubens*, 226.

into the trap of naturalizing grace. In fact, if nature is somehow supernatural, grace is naturalized. In both cases, God's true nature is irrelevant. These are two opposite conclusions, but they are two sides of the same coin, since they both inaccurately describe nature and grace.

The discourse about "pure nature" is important and needs to be revived. Is it not for having put aside such an important hypothesis that not only confusion between nature and grace has arisen in our midst, but also an excellent common doctrine, which is limbo, has been marginalized in the name of God's mercy? The possibility of limbo for unbaptized babies, who died before reaching the age of reason, is a clear manifestation of the consistency of the concept of "pure nature" with all its consequences. Grace is not given unless it is conferred by baptism or, at least, by desiring it. There is no other revelation in the New Testament. Moreover, the desire is indeed personal—not replaceable by that of one of the parents or of loved ones—and it should be a longing for an objective good, baptism, and not a grace already given in nature, disguised under its form. Limbo, where an eternal natural happiness is enjoyed and where no suffering is felt, not even that of the loss of God, manifests the gratuity of grace, its precedence over nature, and its fulfilment of any human desire. Of course it does not do any injustice to babies because grace is never demanded by nature as it due. It can only be a free gift: freely given and freely received.

Hence, the only possible way forward in this theological discussion is to respect the distinction between nature and grace, and above all to accept the mystery of their free and never innate or necessary coordination. Nature is open to grace in virtue of a desire for it, while grace can perfect nature when given by God and freely accepted by man.

One way or the other, in the two theories examined, grace would be given with nature. If this were the case, love should also be required. Anyone can understand that if love is demanded, it is no longer love. Love can only be freely given and freely received. It is the same with grace. We should then appreciate, once again, the intimate conjunction of love and grace. Let's put it now this way: either love and grace go together or they are destined unfortunately to fail together and to leave man even more lonely, alone with his falsely deified nature (the desire to be one's own god) or with his domesticated spiritual life ("know-how" applied even to God). Both are risks of our contemporary culture and both tend toward an atheistic attitude.

Conclusion

"Hail, Full of Grace!"

OUR JOURNEY INTO DISCOVERING the mystery of divine grace has now come to its conclusion. We have tackled various theological questions to enter more deeply into the mystery of divine grace, that mystery so central to our Christian life as well as to theology as such. Divine grace opens up a beautiful horizon of hope: we begin to contemplate the marvels of the Most Holy Trinity in the creation account, which make us clearly understand God's desire for man to find salvation in the mystery of redemption. Creation and redemption are intimately tied up in the unique plan of salvation in Christ (see Eph 1:3–14). Christ is the reason for all things, for all mankind. Christ is the giver of grace, by which we become intimately united with Him, even to the point of sharing in His divine life, being one with the Father and the Holy Spirit, in Him. He made us for one purpose: "to make us praise the glory of his grace" (Eph 1:6). This will be the joy of the elect, who will be saved for all eternity: to sing a "new song" to the Holy Trinity, that "song" of the praise of glory, through the complete transformation by grace.

God's Abode with Man

It is worthwhile to say a final word on our Lady, who is the masterpiece of divine grace. In her, we admire the transformative power of grace, the Woman made grace, and therefore the Lady who gives us grace through her Son, Jesus Christ. The Archangel Gabriel greeted her, saying: "Hail full of grace, the Lord is with thee" (Lk 1:28). The Blessed Virgin is entirely imbued with holy grace. By grace, we mean the divine life poured forth abundantly on her being from her very conception, as well as the numerous favors granted by God. Among many, let us mention her Immaculate Conception—the privilege of being conceived without the stain of sin, the divine Maternity, the virginal espousals to St. Joseph, her role as Co-redemptrix, participating in our salvation as the helpmate of the Redeemer, and finally her role as Mediatrix of All Graces.

Holy Mother Church calls on the Virgin Mary under the title of "Mediatrix of Grace" as well as "Mediatrix of All Graces."[179] These two Marian titles are without doubt

---

[179] In 1921, upon request of Card. Mercier, the primate of Belgium, to define the dogma of our Lady's Universal Mediation, the Holy See granted for Belgium and then for all other dioceses that would request it, the Liturgy for the Holy Mass and Divine Office of "Our Lady Mediatrix of All Graces." The liturgical feast was established on May 8; most of the dioceses celebrated it on May 31, as in England (among the Masses *pro aliquibus locis*). See M. Hauke, *Mary Mediatress of Grace: Mary's Mediation of Grace in the Theological and Pastoral Works of Cardinal Mercier*, Supplement to Mary at the Foot of the Cross IV (Academy of the Immaculate: New Bedford, MA, 2004), 67–77.

intimately bound up, both being consequences of one another. Our Lady is the Mediatrix of grace, and therefore of all graces. Grace, as mentioned before, is the divine life in us. It is a new life, springing up from the redemptive sacrifice of the Lamb. Our Lady gives us this life, because she gave to us the Redeemer Himself, and also because she—as no one else—took an active and unique part in our Redemption, by cooperating personally with Christ as the New Eve, the true Mother of all living.[180]

On Calvary, she is the Woman standing at the foot of the Cross beside the New Adam (see Jn 19:25–27). Her maternal *presence* echoes her *Fiat* at the Annunciation and recapitulates her whole maternal offering for us, her children, in Christ. On that mountain of salvation, we were solemnly declared children of Mary: "Son, behold your Mother." The new life of grace, bought at such a sorrowful price by Christ in union with Mary, began to be diffused through Mary's spiritual maternity. "Woman, behold your son" is the testament of the dying Son, who, from that point onwards, ordains that the fruit of His Redemption must be communicated to all mankind through Mary, through her life-giving maternity.

Mary's spiritual maternity is sacrificial. Her Heart is pierced by a sword. With Christ, she too dies mystically, so that we may be generated to the life of grace. This maternal generation of Christ's mystical body commences from the moment of the Annunciation, growing continuously

[180] Cf *Lumen Gentium* 58, 61–62.

up to the moment on Calvary when all is consummated. This consummation of our Lady's sacrifice is foretold and prefigured by the outstanding lives of several women in the Old Testament, such as Rachel, who dies to give birth to Ben-oni ("son of my sorrow," see Gen 36:16–20), or the mother of the seven Maccabees, who completes the sacrifice of her sons, and at last immolates herself (see 2 Macc 7).

John and all the successive disciples of Christ through the ages would not have access to that salvific mystery save through Mary's maternal mediation. This is the reason for her mediation of grace. The Virgin Mary gives us the grace of salvation, the grace that makes us holy and spotless in God's presence, for she is placed *between* Christ and ourselves, Christ and the Church.

From this mediation of salvific grace, our Lady's role as Mediatrix of all graces takes on a great significance. We may always seek refuge under her mantle, to ask for the graces we need. All treasures are entrusted to her, since the price of our salvation is held safely in her Immaculate Heart, the very "fullness of grace." Mary gives us above all the Holy Spirit. To give us grace means, definitively, to give us the One who sanctifies. As our Lady's presence and greeting sanctified John the Baptist in the womb of Elizabeth (see Lk 1:41), she likewise mediates the presence of her Son when we fly to her, giving us the One who is our Sanctifier and our Consoler. With the entire Church, we entrust ourselves to our Lady, making ours the *Sub tuum praesidium*, one of the oldest Christian prayers addressed the Blessed Virgin Mary:

"Hail, Full of Grace!"

We fly to thy patronage, O holy Mother of God; despise not our petitions in our necessities, but deliver us always from all dangers, O glorious and blessed Virgin. Amen.

You might enjoy some other titles published by Os Justi Press:

DOGMATIC THEOLOGY
Lattey (ed.), *The Incarnation*
Lattey (ed.), *St Thomas Aquinas*
Pohle, *God: His Knowability, Essence, and Attributes*
Pohle, *The Author of Nature and the Supernatural*
Scheeben, *A Manual of Catholic Theology* (2 vols.)
Scheeben, *Nature and Grace*

SPIRITUAL THEOLOGY
Doyle, *Vocations*
Guardini, *Sacred Signs*
Leen, *The True Vine and Its Branches*
Swizdor, *God in Me*

LITURGY
A Benedictine Martyrology
The Life of Worship
The Roman Martyrology (Pocket Edition)
Chaignon, *The Sacrifice of the Mass Worthily Offered*
Croegaert, *The Mass: A Liturgical Commentary* (2 vols.)
Kwasniewski (ed.), *John Henry Newman on Worship,*
Reverence, and Ritual
Parsch, *The Breviary Explained*
Pothier, *Cantus Mariales*
Shaw, *Sacred and Great*

LANGUAGE & LITERATURE
The Little Flowers of Saint Francis (illustrated)
Brittain, *Latin in Church*
Farrow, *Pageant of the Popes*
Kilmer, *Anthology of Catholic Poets*
Lazu Kmita, *The Island Without Seasons*
Papini, *Gog*
Walsh, *The Catholic Anthology*